Gayatri Jayaraman is a Mumbai-based editor and writer. She has over 19 years of experience in journalism, working on an intersectional study of social trends as impacted by politics, economics and culture. She has worked with India Today and Mint Lounge and has written extensively across digital and traditional media. She grew up in Lagos, Nigeria, and Kodaikanal, South India. She is a single mother to a 16-year-old son, Dhruv, and lives in Thane with her German Shepherd mix, Zitto. This is her debut work of non-fiction.

WHO ME, POOR?

WHO ME, POOR?

How India's youth are living in urban
poverty to make it big

Gayatri Jayaraman

BLOOMSBURY
NEW DELHI • LONDON • OXFORD • NEW YORK • SYDNEY

First published in India 2017

© 2017 by Gayatri Jayaraman

All rights reserved. No part of this publication may be reproduced or transmitted in any form or by any means, electronic or mechanical, including photocopying, recording, or any information storage or retrieval system, without prior permission in writing from the publishers.

No responsibility for loss caused to any individual or organization acting on or refraining from action as a result of the material in this publication can be accepted by Bloomsbury or the author.

The content of this book is the sole expression and opinion of its author, and not of the publisher. The publisher in no manner is liable for any opinion or views expressed by the author. While best efforts have been made in preparing this book, the publisher makes no representations or warranties of any kind and assumes no liabilities of any kind with respect to the accuracy or completeness of the content and specifically disclaims any implied warranties of merchantability or fitness of use for a particular purpose.

The publisher believes that the content of this book does not violate any existing copyright/intellectual property of others in any manner whatsoever. However, in case any source has not been duly attributed, the publisher may be notified in writing for necessary action.

BLOOMSBURY and the Diana logo are trademarks of Bloomsbury Publishing Plc

ISBN 978 93 86432 23 0
2 4 6 8 10 9 7 5 3 1

Bloomsbury Publishing India Pvt. Ltd
Second Floor, LSC Building No.4
DDA Complex, Pocket C – 6 & 7, Vasant Kunj
New Delhi 110070
www.bloomsbury.com

Typeset by Manipal Digital Systems
Printed and bound in India by Thomson Press India Ltd.

To find out more about our authors and books visit www.bloomsbury.com. Here you will find extracts, author interviews, details of forthcoming events and the option to sign up for our newsletters.

For Dhruv,
and all that we spent together

Contents

SECTION I: Who Me, Poor?

₹1. The Hungry
Who for his greed, who for his hunger, who shall I say is calling? Leonard Cohen 3

₹2. The Homeless
To be without a home, like a complete unknown, Like a rolling stone Bob Dylan 29

₹3. The Driven
Oh Lord, won't you buy me a Mercedes Benz? My friends all drive Porsches, I must make amends. Janis Joplin 42

₹4. The Boundary-less
Freedom's just another word for nothing left to lose Janis Joplin 52

SECTION II: Why We Spend

₹5. Expensive Degrees
Oh, I know our troubles will be gone, goin' gone If we dream, dream, dream for free. Patti Smith 65

₹6. Exploitative Workplaces
But if you ask for a rise it's no surprise that they're giving none away Pink Floyd 73

₹7. Easy Money
I went to my brother to ask for a loan cause
I was busted Ray Charles.. 89

₹8. Evolving City
A working class hero is something to be If you want
to be a hero, just follow me John Lennon 94

SECTION III: Brand 'I'

₹9. Occupational Shift
Do you want to make tea at the BBC? The Clash 105

₹10. Generational Shift
Can you pick up all the pieces of this
broken generation? Of Mice & Men 117

₹11. Paradigm Shift
Them Belly Full (But We Hungry) Bob Marley 129

₹12. New Identity
Y'all don't know my struggle Y'all can't match
my hustle Kanye West 143

SECTION IV: Go for Broke

₹13. Rentals & Freebies
The stupid things that you do because you think
that poor is cool Pulp 161

₹14. Financial Literacy
Everything's gonna be fine fine fine 'cause I've
got one hand in my pocket And the other one is
giving a high five Alanis Morisette 171

Acknowledgements   **183**

SECTION I
Who Me, Poor?

The Hungry – The Homeless –
The Driven – The Boundary-less

₹1.

The Hungry

Who For His Greed, Who For His Hunger, Who Shall I Say Is Calling? Leonard Cohen

Love in times of hunger

Saurav Srivastav, 26, MBA, IT sales, New Delhi

The problem most guys face on Tinder, they'll tell you, is that women get all the responses, more than they need, and men get almost none. Even if someone matches with you, they send monosyllabic responses and string you along — if you are an average-looking, average-earning guy like most of us are — until all her other crushes have been exhausted. So, I was really surprised when this not-bad-looking woman not only matched with me but messaged me, gave me her cellphone number and wanted to meet that very night itself. I was in Gurgaon, and though she also lived around 20 minutes away, I was just back from office, and it seemed odd, to rush somewhere at 10 PM at night, so I tried to put it off. But she insisted we meet at the Subway near her house. So, again, I said 'maybe tomorrow'. Then she said: "Can you ask them to deliver?" So, I asked why she couldn't just order it herself. She said she would have but her credit card was maxed out and her debit card didn't have enough balance. She was hungry. I cut the call, blocked her and deleted the app. Freeloaders.

◆◆◆

Broke is a romantic state of being when you are coming of age. The prevalent rags-to-riches fantasy conjures a vision of leaving from home, quite penniless, with one backpack, and making a tangible, commercial impact in the tough, wide world on the force of one's brilliant ideas, one's face aflush with the glow of always-around-the-corner success.

It's only a year later, well into the post-honeymoon period of a dream opening in a coveted industry, that you realise clothes crumple in backpacks. And not only does the corporate world not think much of those who show up to meetings in crumpled clothes, but that those mundane trappings—a well-tailored jacket, a high-end laptop, jumping into an expensive cab so you can get to a meeting on time, which perfume or body spray or mist lingers when you exit an elevator or a boardroom, how 'put together' you look with your ironed out hair, which superhero T-shirt to wear to a Sunday team outing, or in which cool pub you waved breezily at an important client—might snag you a better 'in' with your boss and mark you out ahead of the rat race. The clichés, the pieces of the mental image this job sells you, you realise with growing horror, exist for a reason. They make you feel more confident, and induct you into a system that comes pre-validated. Upon these foundations, the hierarchy of ascent is built.

It is the survival of the fittest. The networkers build contacts that guarantee visibility and ease their way into the next job. The well-groomed bag the ritziest client list. The articulate and the hip get pushed to populate the front row. The worker ants get respect, but make no money and rarely bag coveted designations. The supervisors get weeded out on either people skills or productivity and will only go so far on either one wheel. On the other hand, the team player who is also a hard taskmaster—one who enthusiastically joins in the big team lunch after the slog fest to meet an impossible deadline—will be around long after you've made your fortune elsewhere. The job jumpers may seem unstable now, but they're the ones who will create value. And the stick-in-the-muds, who are too afraid to risk, become foundation stones so that others may. Some do and never get noticed, while others sell themselves over their skills. 'Maverick' works within specific boundaries. Of course there are exceptions, and exceptional bosses, but just like relationships and *He's Just Not That Into You*, the exception is never the rule. And you increasingly need to pick your groove early on.

Finding one's place within this ecosystem is as little a choice as human nature will allow. In Steven Pinker's 2002 treatise, *The Blank Slate: The Modern Denial of Human Nature*, the psychologist points to four fears that propel us: the first is a fear of inequality, followed by the fears of imperfectability, determinism, and nihilism. That we will not become perfect, over-achievers due to biological factors, due to factors external to us, and due to a lack of continuity, propel us. The need to belong, and paradoxically, supersede the environment one belongs to, is ingrained. Striving, then, becomes at once a belonging and a rising above. Those wins mean nothing unless they are lauded within the group. No one wants to create a breakthrough invention or application and leave it in a forest. It must be hailed as a breakthrough within the circuit we exist in. The new work place becomes almost a microcosm of these fears in play.

It is systemically built up. Those questions they asked you at entry point—what your parents do, the number of siblings, what educational institutions you claim alumni status at, which neighbourhood address you now rent in—are not quite so innocuous. These are tailored to filter and reward an essential fitting in. "Are you cut from our cloth?" they seem to ask. And whether you choose to fit in or break out will in turn tailor your rewards accordingly, in the now or in the distant future. For many whose ascent to a corporate career is in itself a breaking out—of previous class barriers, small town milieus, educational, social, financial, or cultural disadvantages—few are able to choose to break out further. The status quo itself becomes the aspirational. You are already, even as you evaluate these choices of where to fit in, and what kind of groove will work for you, inducted, a link into the larger chain. You pick a choice that was never quite yours to make.

In the meanwhile, the cost of it becomes increasingly apparent. It dawns on you that the only glow you will ever get while sweating it out in overly air-conditioned cubicles with harsh lighting that leaves your skin craving sunlight and fresh air, is from a facial you can't afford. The spirited leap into adulthood, you discover, is not so much about going down the rabbit hole uninhibited, but more about escaping the Red Queen and getting home through the nightmarish Looking Glass where tea time in the conference room is but a Mad Hatter's party in which everyone is vying for the same chair and more than willing to drink from the same cup.

Should you seek out a coffee to take the edge off, what is immediately available is a terrible acidity-inducing reconstituted office machine variety. Should you happen to work in a swank glass edifice in a newly-gentrified locale, succumbing to a 200 rupee coffee results in—not the caffeine keeping you awake—the steep daily cost steadily piling up like a game of Trellis gone wild on your credit card. As the bills mount—a team lunch, that occasional coffee, an Uber every time you're late—the minimum amount due begins to bleed into the monthly salary. A day comes when you wistfully consider food delivery service Zomato's taunting discount code: 'BROKE', that's hitherto been landing in the Spam folder. There is, by now, a proportionately growing pit in your stomach that no street side cheap lunch can cure.

Should you fail to meet that month's minimum due, which you most likely will, you tell yourself there is no point beating yourself up for having succumbed to one coffee a day, one night at a movie or eating well, when you, unthinking fool you, sought human company. If you can't take a cab home once a week, why are you working this hard anyway? Isn't the thought of this lifestyle what motivated you through every competitive exam? Now, momentary indulgences bring punishment, you realise. As a consequence, you impose on yourself a vice tax amongst the long list of others that you no longer comprehend, appended to your carefully miscalculated bill, now inflated beyond your least conservative estimate. You will have one of two choices — borrow and make the payment now, or rotate the interest and the late payment penalty to the next month, when you will have more money, and will be more sensible, you vow to yourself (mother promise). Both are the wrong answer. You will realise this when your credit card maxes itself out after many months of hitting upon the wrong answer.

For now, you sleep, belly full and soul satiated with the idyllic promise of ambition. You are young and show promise and the company promised you a raise if you perform well. Except, they promised that to all the new joinees around you, 40 per cent of whom will not make it to the four year mark, when, on average, the company filters out those they value enough to bet their monies on. According to the Deloitte Millenial Survey 2016, in any case, they expect two-thirds of you want to leave long before they have to hand you out any more money. Everyone's a big believer in evolution in corporate circles. When the natural filtration process is done, they'll decide whom to promote then. It'll be a while.

But as usual, the older generation is only measuring the tangibles. You are young, and you are borrowing not just from future income but future hope in your ability to win big. Never mind that you have already spent the raise you have not yet received. You are building an image on the kind of success you want to be. An image you have of yourself reading in coffee shops, travelling the world, clicking selfies at that new restobar in town that's so cool it has jars for glasses, and being liked and RTed on social media so much that your (latest-model) smartphone cannot stop pinging in meetings and your boss, so aware of how well-rounded your sparkling personality is, gestures to you to put it on silent. It is never enough to succeed; it is important how you do so.

It will be some time before you learn to tread water. For now, as the bills begin to pour in, and this emerging adulthood is a staying afloat, head above water, resisting that anchor of iron responsibility weighing you to the sea bed. You came here without a life jacket, and without learning how to swim either. The water level meets your nose. There is no cashback for the lifestyle you've bought yourself in exchange for the cash that should have gone towards that electricity bill. The image you bought from magazines, those sports shoes that made you feel healthy on the two occasions you used them, don't fetch anything in sales — God knows you've tried — and there is no hotfooting it to another island paradise vacation instead. Because tomorrow is another bill.

Adulthood is paying your dues.

You are not alone

This is the cost of aspiration. The underbelly of the 'consumer economy' that everyone is always gung-ho about. There is a being left behind, but there is also the confidence of catching up.

Every few years, the People's Research on India's Consumer Economy (PRICE) conducts a survey. In 2014, while studying India's attitudes towards cash, Rama Bijapurkar, Rajesh Shukla and Mridusmita Bordoloi found that "cash is seen to be a means of control and discipline over spending", also noting that "most developed economies with high degrees of financial inclusion are characterised by low usage of cash as a medium of exchange".

With a more fluid class mobility, migration rises. Chief Economic Advisor Arvind Subramanian in his Economic Survey 2016-17 estimates that nine million migrants travel between states for work. Over the last 15 years, the disparity between richer and poorer states is also rising, contrary to what's happening in countries like China, he points out. People with aspirations are moving across the country to fulfil them and moves like demonetisation are pushing the cashless economy. Moved into the credit economy, this opens them up to gain access to new banking instruments like the emerging payday loans that extend small amounts to people who just need to get through to the end of the month, and Line of Credit loans, where instalments only include interest, allowing for deferred payment of the principal. These are all driving decisions about relocation, work and lifestyle—when you move to a new city without substantial savings or a sound financial backer today, where once you bummed a loan from an uncle, you are more likely to think of taking a small loan to tide you over and help you settle in. Today, there is a rising confidence in one's ability to take credit, earn, and pay back in the future.

Credit cards are seeing an unprecedented growth, hitting 32 per cent in 2017. Credit card usage is linked to high consumer confidence levels. In the 2014 PRICE survey, three-fourth of users claimed high confidence. Even so, at the time, credit cards had penetrated only a small segment of progressives, i.e. the affluent, the educated, the salaried: 19.3 per cent of graduates, 36.4 per cent of post graduates, and 14.9 per cent of the salaried owned credit cards. Around 23 per cent were between 21 and 30 years of age, and 57 per cent of them were salaried. Among household assets, while television, cable connection, two-wheelers and refrigerators had penetrated all types of consumer categories, cars, air conditioners, laptops and the Internet had penetrated mostly among credit card owners. Through the credit card, connectivity and confidence are acquired.

In a parallel study on *Middle India: Key to Inclusive Growth and a Prosperous Future India*, PRICE looked at a true Middle India—the middle 60 per cent of households by income—164 million households, only 16 per cent of whose wage earners are graduates and who save only 7.7 per cent of household income. The group found a rising confidence in them, an optimism to be included, though 69 per cent said they met their basic needs with great difficulty.

In 2016, PRICE's 'Household Survey on India's Citizen Environment & Consumer Economy found that more than a quarter of Indian households incur debt, most to informal sources. Twenty seven per cent have at least one outstanding loan with a median outstanding of 50,000 rupees in metros, boom towns and niche cities, and 12 per cent have informal loans.

A National Sample Survey Office (NSSO) survey in 2013 showed 22.4 per cent of households incurred debt. All surveys, private or public, typify typical households and neglect to count young migrants, those with no permanent addresses and no identifiable householder status.

And yet, we are repeatedly told our economy, the much-promised boom that is to come, depends entirely on their shoulders, these millennials, estimated to be 28 per cent of the Indian population, and their ability and susceptibility to be enticed to spend. "Millennials are the creators of the new economy", former MySpace's CEO Mike Jones put it. With a per capita income of $2,400, and forming 28 per cent of the Indian population, they will drive online transactions in India, Parag Gupta, Executive Director for Technology, Internet and Media, Morgan Stanley, said last year. Over 73 per cent of millennials part of a BBC Advertising survey conducted by Voxpopme in September 2016 said they were intensely brand conscious.

The millennials will drive our economy. What no one is telling them is that they, both beneficiary and victim to this promised boom, are its fuel.

"I drink water and go to bed"

Tanvi Jain, 24, Journalist, Mumbai

Last night, I drank water and went to bed. My first meal today was at 6 PM and it was a streetside sandwich. This is my first real job with a newspaper. I used to work in a wire agency back home in New Delhi, but I used to live with my parents there. My edition closes at midnight and by the time I get home it is 1 AM. I have neither the energy nor the equipment to cook and so every meal involves eating out. Towards the last week of the month, I just don't have money so I go without eating. People think I am frivolous but most of my salary goes in rent, commuting, clothes and eating out. I don't buy branded clothes, I try to buy off the street, but everything in Mumbai is expensive and adds up. One set of new clothes, one cab ride, one nice meal and it feels like you are being punished sometimes. In your first job, if you want to grow, you have to show up looking half decent, there are times you have to show up on time, or go to a meal at a place which you ordinarily on your own wouldn't enter. If I have to make friends in a new city, I have to buy the kind of dresses and shoes that are suitable for clubs and restaurants. If I do not, what is the point of coming here and earning and finding a new life? Why not have some fun, find some friends, possibly love, while doing it? It's not a choice; it's an investment in fitting in.

This dilemma dates back to 2009 when I moved out of my home town for the first time to pursue further studies. Excited for the new college, new city, new people, independence, the excitement drained out when it came to managing finances. I belong to a middle class family and my parents used to send Rs 2,000 per month for living in a city like Delhi. Although the amount wasn't enough to fulfil my basic needs but for us, the urban poor, comfort and luxury are more important. Also with new friends around, you feel like partying every other day and that's what I ended up doing. We would go out somewhere or the other every single day, and of course, to keep it fair everyone had to contribute equally as well. Within a couple of days, my Facebook account was full of happening pictures, Likes, comments, etc. But who knows the reality? That no matter how much we spend with our friends, when it comes to spending on ourselves, on a basic meal, on something healthy, that's where we compromise the most because we know if we spend here, we won't be left with enough money to spend in parties. It was a horrible scenario, and even now, after seven years, when I am earning, not a lot has changed, as the expenses have increased accordingly. There have been times I have slept with an empty stomach or managed with snacks my mother packed for me when I left the house, but when it comes to spending in restaurants or clubs, I am up for it. It seems like a never-ending story as initially I used to think that once I start earning, my life will be sorted, but not much has changed so far except that now I don't bother my parents for money. However, I am still an urban poor and considering the pace at which our expenses are increasing with time, I think this scenario won't end any time soon. No matter how much I earn, I don't think things will change. I will still end up going to bed hungry, because nothing is enough to keep up.

♦♦♦

In the summer of 2000, I joined a fashion magazine as the chief of the Hyderabad bureau. When a decomposing marriage brought me back to Mumbai, I transferred to the Mumbai office and was now working at a Hyderabad remuneration in a much more expensive city. My salary before taxes was Rs 10,000. The editor, then a monopolist in the trade, would induct me into her entourage while she did the rounds of major fashion designers' stores. At Ritu Kumar's at the Oberoi shopping centre, she would point to a small shelf in the corner and breezily suggest I pick out one from the discount section. Even with a 40 per cent discount, the Ritu Kumar pant suit—a fashionable orange and green outfit with a matching silk scarf was ill-suited to a 26-year-old mother with financial and marriage pressures and commuting by local train from Thane. An ensemble that cost Rs 4,000 was more than three quarters of my monthly salary. In the days of Shopper's Stop mix-and-match kurtas being the only upgrade you hit after Fashion Street, this was quite the monetary leap in terms of apparel. The conversation would quickly go from "it's lovely, but it's not for me" to "I can't quite afford it" and landslide into "I'll pay for it, you pay me when you have the money" behind forced plastic smiles. When your boss in your first or second job piles the pressure on like that, whether you have the money or not and whether your husband is yelling bloody murder or not about the finances, you go home, pull the Rs 4,000 out and fork it over. It happened twice by the time I began to search for another job, with other factors than needing to shop accelerating my need for better pay. My next job gave me a 150 per cent hike in salary, bumping it up to Rs 25,000. But the damage had already been done. Several items I would never need again, from clothes and jewellery to expensive lunches, taken to fit in to a field where earning a salary seemed incidental to most thriving in it, were already on my credit card and had dented any potential savings. By this time, I had moved out on my own, which also meant taking a personal loan to put down a deposit, which meant an Equated Monthly Instalment (EMI) equal to rent, childcare, a new office in Andheri, which meant commute costs, sometimes exacerbated by the need to rush back home through Saki Naka traffic before the crèche closed, besides utility bills, and groceries. The rolled over credit card bills were denting me. I had no furniture but two mattresses on the ground, a small radio, and a few kitchen utensils that included a knife with which to flip dosas. My limited gold stash was long sold, but thank God, there were two Ritu Kumars in the suitcase I was living out of. As the minimum amount due mounted, and I scrimped on the oil and wheat, so did the farce of hope.

Pocket Pressure

The episode left me with a healthy disrespect for insidious ways in which people in positions of power induct you consciously or thoughtlessly into their own financial agendas and spending patterns. It also taught me that what you assume to be just a matter of stretching your income to meet your ends — most young people who find themselves severely in debt will tell you they started out assuming it was 'a phase' that would end once their income rose as it inevitably would — doesn't quite even itself out as salaries rise. The more income rises, the higher the expenses to earn it become. A financial backlog, much like a few grams of chocolate that miraculously become kilograms of love handles, stretches itself out.

Putting oneself into this kind of long-term debt is mesmerisingly like watching sticky taffy twist into a Mobius loop on the turning machine — sticky, stringy and its multi-coloured strands intertwined into the sweet promise of a treat. But should you stop, and not handle it right, it'll just be a giant, twisted mess — a Pocket Twist. It's, therefore, not just an equation of income to expense. The math isn't that simple, and if it were, several would be able to step out of debt as easily as they get into it: by simply switching the machine off. It's a bit more complex than that. That the machine is on at all is a function of many more whys: your sweet tooth, the dependability of the sweet tooth of several around you, the taffy vendor and his need to make a living off you, and the entire exercise of marketability, a whole fairground replete with ensnaring lights and tantalising music.

The taffy doesn't, in fact, you learn in time, exist in isolation. And you're getting cavities.

This Pocket Twist, a state of ensnarement, propagates through a number of factors. First, a lack of self-assertion is in itself a tangible cost. In a first job or two, new joinees are rarely able to say 'no' to expected behaviours without the fear of walking away unscathed. Everyone spends at their personal level of financial accountability, and the idea that there is a 'collective' standard for the outcome of that individual spending becomes problematic. The expectations of what contributes to your professional image within the bracket of your personal ambition are sown here.

Second, starter salaries do not dress you for the job you want, they dress you for the job you have. This is often the first job you've been offered and is sold to you on the idea that you are lucky enough to even be part of the work force, so take what comes. All vulnerabilities — social, financial, sexual — begin here, particularly financial, regardless of your industry of operation. Whether in the film industry or in a start-up, salary negotiation and the living wage are rarely considered. Getting a foot in is not priceless.

Third, living on one's own brings a plethora of practical expenses that are difficult for anyone who hasn't lived alone before to navigate. Unlike the US or Europe, there is no gap year, sabbatical or pre-set pattern of young people setting up that one follows. Every striking out is a lone journey. There is a real cost applicable to starting out with no assets, no family, or community backing.

Fourth, every rupee you miss on the dreaded credit card EMI is akin to stepping into a quicksand bar to cross a rapidly rising river; credit card use is not for those who do not understand how its interest application works. Few do. The push to a cashless economy without crucial education and financial literacy—which is much more than simply showing people where to sign or how to use an ATM work—is half an education.

And fifth, investing in self-pride to get past loneliness and social isolation is a cost society never quite factors in. These translate, quite simply, into palpable influencers: brand 'I', the living wage, the changing impact of migration, financial literacy, and social net worth.

These influencers affect people differently. In the same workplace, I had a senior, who, when asked if she would come out for a fancy team lunch, would retort, all the while laughing, "if I had Rs 500 to spare, why would I spend it on you rather than my husband and child?" There was yet another who was called a 'sadak chhap' (of the street/road) journalist for wearing an inelegant pair of sandals to work and who was immensely wounded by it. Why does one set of stated employer financial values not imprint on one subordinate, but does on another? Often, factors like line of reporting, years of work experience, seniority, and the aspiration for professional approval come into play. It's also where you are in your career and personal life: at some stages you are vying more keenly for institutional, family, and societal approval than in others, where you are yourself primed to hit a breakout phase.

It is also the endorsement of expected work behaviour, rewards and punishment, meted out to those who do and do not comply that set a standard. Is someone who shows up in a less compliant brand of fancy footwear being berated? Are those who are the best dressed also the best rewarded when it comes to appraisals? Corporate culture revolves around rewarding team players and office workspaces have not yet evolved into places where diversity goes beyond the token. The outlier is not the standard for deviation.

There are also personal choices—some poor, some strategic—along with upbringing, aesthetic sensibility, milieu, and luck that impact you. Everyone processes their environment differently depending on who they are and what they're made of.

The result of not being able to live within one's income is personally crippling and professionally stunting. There are some who skip meals, who spend entire meetings afraid to sip coffee at a client meet lest they be asked to pay for it, and others whose productivity is impacted by wondering if they have to walk home that night. Those who manage to dodge the expenses are often consciously penalised by the environment, or end up leading depressingly isolated lives. While it is easy to dismiss several of these predicaments as poor financial literacy or bad choice, often it is perceived as a lack of choice by those who are in the position to exercise it. In the cross-hairs of that trap is the denouement.

These are accentuated by systemic lacunae—from a lack of affordable public housing, to crowded and unwieldy transport systems, the gentrification of lower income housing and work localities in the name of municipal beautification that drives out cheaper eating and purchase options, free public spaces where individuals may enjoy leisure time without additional expenses, and indeed, a work culture that does not see value in leisure—thus, pushing the working class mass into bottled and marketed ideas of what an ideal work day and work play looks like.

The idea of success in our heads — what it ought to look like and its signifiers — are largely peer-ordained. How we define success determines what we move towards and how.

"I was so emaciated, I fit right in"

Shweta Ratnakar, 27, Fashion Assistant, Mumbai, from coastal Karnataka

When I first came here as a student out of NIFT (National Institute of Fashion Technology, Ahmedabad), I stayed in Khargar. But when I started working full-time with a fashion house in town, more than Khargar not being cool enough, it was socially isolating from the industry that I hoped to build a career in. The commute to town was also too long for me. So, I moved to Bandra where many of my classmates were living. We four girls rented a one one-bedroom apartment and paid rents of Rs 25,000 each. My salary was Rs 35,000 and the rest would go in electricity and mobile bills and commuting. Also, working in an industry like fashion you have to turn up well-groomed. You have to network with designers and clientèle that knows the best brands in the business from experience. If you have the fortune to have been to one of the top fashion institutes in the country, and are assistant to a top design house, it's just not an option to show up at work in salwar-kurtas and chappals. Fashion requires you to dress a certain way, and that requires an expensive investment in clothes, accessories and grooming. You have to convince your employers and their clients equally that you know what good styling is. Fashion was my dream, and I do not come from a wealthy family. My mother single-handedly raised three of us on the earnings of a small-town bank job. I was given the opportunity to pursue my ambitions, even though the fees were a burden on her. As the eldest, now that I had made it this far, I could not back down and go try something else more lucrative and less socially pressuring. I had to not just work with what resources I had, I had to ensure that I rose in my career and made a success of it. So I bought the clothes I needed, and attended the parties and dinners that required me to network and be noticed in the industry. What I compromised on instead was food. I lived off vadapavs, which cost me Rs 5 a day, and soon enough, I got a stomach infection. Because of the infection I couldn't eat anything for a while. I didn't have money for doctors and soon it turned into a full-blown eating disorder. I would keep telling people who offered to go to lunch with me that I was on a very specific diet and I consequently began to lose a lot of weight. That's common in the looks-based industry we are in, so nobody questioned it too much. I couldn't afford to have all this known back home, where they were convinced I was on my way to my dream life. I gradually stopped visiting my relatives in Mumbai whom I used to initially visit once a week when I first moved here. They would have alerted my family. By the time my uncle came over one day to find out why I had stopped going over to visit them, he found me so emaciated that he had to carry me down the three flights of stairs in his arms. I was a skeleton.

♦♦♦

The Hungry Tide

Food has always been a basic prop to the working man's lot. The waves of migration in the 1950s and 1960s brought mill workers from the Konkan coast, Goa, Tamil Nadu and Gujarat to Mumbai. With each one came the growth of street food, music, community theatre, community dwellings in areas like the Tamilian Matunga, Gujarati Ghatkopar, and Goan Kalbadevi. As the collective rose, it carried the individual with it. Along with these came the rise of street food stalls—cheap eats sold by hawkers at the time, bhaji with pav substituting the roti as an easy and warm hand-held eat, cut fruits on hand carts, buttermilk, boiled eggs, and bhel, the kebabs on charcoal grills down Mohammed Ali Road to feed the dock workers, peak times being when the dock, mill, railways and factory workers would end their shifts. The Shiv Sena tried to politically capitalise on this food currency with its Zunka Bhakar stalls in the mid 1980s, making the ubiquitous Udupi restaurant the focus of its attacks. The Udupis had brought simple hygienic 'tiffin' services to the streets of Mumbai and every subsequent incoming wave—from Tibetans selling momos to resettled refugees from Sindh setting up parantha lanes and gallis in settlements today that once grew out of camps—is testament to how integral food is to the socio-economic migrant.

In New Delhi, a city formed by repeated migrations through history, and which, even today, bears the burden of the maximum inter-state migration in the country, street food becomes integral to the survival of the mutable masses who settle in Jhuggi Jhopri clusters and unauthorised colonies, and satellite towns like Gurgaon, where residents have to largely come up with their own arrangements for infrastructure. In these newer spaces, the availability of food becomes a foraging, one that apps and new take-out joints are capitalising on, rather than an established system. In the 'hyperlocal' ecosystem, food delivery services, food tech companies, and ordering plus delivery platforms, have been the first and the biggest to want in on the urban India growth story. Their target audience is the increasingly hungry tide that has forgotten, or forgoes, communal eating to become individualised units of success.

Why migration today operates in a vacuum is best understood by how much of a community activity it once was.

Almost forensically, settlements in Mumbai trace back to a process of migration that was heavily community-influenced with new workers arriving in the city on the basis of missives sent back by members of their family or their village, on what work and accommodation was available in the city and at what cost. In a New Delhi racked repeatedly by the riots of Partition and communal violence, the Sikh pogrom of 1984, migrations tended to keep subsequent generations within tight clusters, linguistic and ethnic. There has always been something very tribal and primal about how we relocated ourselves, as though we carried with us a memory of motion imprinted in our DNA since the first movements out of the Indus Valley. The baton was passed to a next generation heading out into the unknown. Much of how cultural traditions — oral histories, food, music, and language — have been preserved has to do with this knitting of a pattern to what was passed down.

Despite the Internet, migration has never been so blind and unthinking an intrusion historically, as it is today. In Dhobi Talao, over 200 Goan kudds, resembling the villages to which the migrant members belonged, were established. These were places that provided cheap accommodation, where men could get a mattress, home-cooked food, and share a sense of community with others like themselves, enjoying a game of football, or a record on the club turnstile, watch some television, while they did their day jobs. The kudds helped set up in the new city. It provided them with common resources — things like lockers for valuables, or an iron to press their clothes, even the picture or a statue of a village patron saint to provide them the bonding of religion. In Matunga, it was the South Indian mess, where young bachelors could eat a complete rice plate for a few rupees. Working men's hostels performed vital roles in assimilation into a city's work and social culture. A few working women's hostels sprung up, but their growth has not kept pace with the needs of the times (today there are around five working women's hostels of repute in each of the metros, insufficient for the larger working populace). More than just fading sepia-toned landmark institutions as perceived today, these clubs performed a crucial function for the city of migrants — it kept the incoming crowd tethered to home-cooked meals and a sense of where they came from. The new waves of migrants, often themselves second-generation migrants from the cities where they leave nuclear families behind onward to newer shores to become sub-nuclear or atomic units without moorings, have no such anchorage in community and hence, nothing to steady themselves with before they set out to stabilise themselves with their earnings.

The newbie white collar worker builds his skyscraper without any scaffolding.

"We once cooked together"

Manoj Harit, 50, Advocate, Malegaon and Mumbai

Marwadis used to have places called wadis in and around the Kalbadevi area. Few still remain. It was a wonderful ecosystem where everyone was given a small place of ten square feet in which they would sleep, live and stack their cooking vessels. One member of the wadi would cook in the morning and evening by turns. Very little money was charged. Many successful Marwadis, who are millionaires today, with apartments in Malabar Hill, started their lives in these wadis. My father was one of them. His first salary was Rs 50 a month working for the Siyaram Silk Mill. He was staying in one of the wadis when the company, which wanted to utilise the power looms in Malegaon, asked if he would relocate to Malegaon village for three to four years. They raised his pay to Rs 100. In time he started his own brokerage firm and a manufacturing unit that spanned 100 acres employing 300 workers. He built his life from those wadis. I too lived in the Modern Hindu Hotel, another relic of this era, where I would get food and accommodation for Rs 250 until seven to eight years ago. I loved it because it provided simple home-cooked food, the amenities were not fancy but neat and clean, and it also formed an ecosystem—you got to meet people from around Maharashtra and South India who visited the city on work. These places, which once provided cheap, hygienic and supportive infrastructure for migrants, are dying out today.

♦♦♦

Lobbies of five star hotels in Indian metros are filled with young men in off-the-rack jackets and young women in off-and-online-sale skirt suits awaiting client meetings. Some of them, in client services, have an expense account for such activities and the company reimburses them for a reasonable number of coffees or teas or sandwiches that become inevitable during the course of the conversation. Most don't. "In fact, it's the only reason I got myself a credit card at all. But even then they only reimburse it at the end of the month. But my credit card due date is 24th, and my salary only comes on the 2nd or 3rd, so already by the time I can even make a minimum payment, the amount has attracted late charges, and nobody reimburses those. Also, somehow no matter what you do, money that you have spent never comes back to fill the gap at the end of the month. It's always less," said Manoj Sharma, a 25-year-old marketing executive in a tech firm, waiting in the lobby of the Taj Lands' End. Sharma is waiting to meet a client who had kindly offered to introduce him to another businessman who was newly setting up shop, and therefore, offered him the opportunity to make a large sale. He hadn't eaten at all that day, as he was saving the space on his card for any cost that would accrue from the meeting. He had some cash, but even that was back up "in case the card fails". When you do not come from privilege, and have not paid your minimum due for a few months, reality is the sound of a credit card being declined.

I ask if it hasn't struck him that the profit from the potential sale would go in actual terms to the office inventory. It only notionally applies to him, the executive, for having made the sale. But the cost of the coffee, present in the here and now, is a very tangible cost to be paid. "The effort will be considered in my appraisals at the end of the year", Sharma shrugs, with a smile. If he doesn't make the sale, that's just one more expensive coffee that he paid for that went nowhere. It seems like a small risk, though for him, with Rs 22,000 salary and rent to pay, it is a very big one indeed, but one he is willing to take. He sees it as an investment. "We have to go out of our way and set up these meetings or we will not grow", he says. He points out that the company only profits if he actually makes a sale, but he profits from the work experience made available to him, and when he exits, that is what will stay with him. I leave him unable to decide whether he is foolishly naive, or brave and intelligent.

Young people everywhere are investing in this notional profit for their future. The bill will come at the end of the month and is not reimbursable because it is a coffee poured of his initiative. He hopes his boss will be fair to him, but if he isn't, he is preparing himself to gain what he needs from his work experience, and move on. So, are the young awake and smelling the coffee, or intoxicated by it?

Several stories like these pour in from around the country. Two marketing managers from New Delhi speak of going hungry since they may have to pay for coffee in the evening. A medical representative speaks of walking up to 15 kilometres a day to save on taxi and rickshaw fares that eat into his salary. A finance manager in an multi-national firm mentions travelling to work by hitching rides on passing trucks and surviving on one meal a day. A publisher tells the story of a young visitor who would hang around till he was offered breakfast. The first port of compromise when the month outlasts the money is always food.

Hunger is a great leveller. Hunger is not a competition; it is equally painful, physically and psychologically, to all who face it. Hunger, and with it poverty, becomes a spectrum, with the intensity of it varying, rather than an absolute, in which some are dubbed unworthy of the pain of their experience. These distinctions are often mixed with the complex politics of the non-governmental organisation ready with a cheque of dole to cash, in the wake of which entire swathes of people get labelled as 'worthy of aid'. The question is not the same as 'worthy of feeling hunger'—a confusion that stems from deep-rooted class issues and hierarchies of control over them.

Aid workers tend to confuse the two. All human beings are 'worthy' of hunger, the range and depth varying. Only some may be worthy of a specific kind of aid, however.

The need to change the way we look at the problems thrown up by various kinds of poverty was brought home to me most powerfully by Dr Devi Shetty. Dr Shetty, India's greatest cardio surgeon and the man behind the $800 heart surgery model, now a United Nations case study on how to replicate affordable cardiac care across developing and developed nations like the UK whose systems are in a perpetual state of inadequacy, sat behind his ebony desk in the Narayana Hrudayalaya in Anekal, Bangalore. Patient after patient filed in to be reassured that not only were their tickers in fine hands, but that their families would not be burdened by the costs that would be left behind for them, should such a surgery fail. Shetty says he spent the years he was studying, envying the West. "Someday", he heard his seniors and teachers say, "India will be a wealthy country, and then we will have good medical care". And it seemed as if all of India was waiting for that promised future to begin. Yet, as he began to work and travel, he realised that wealthy countries themselves struggle with the cost of affordable healthcare. That's when it clicked, he says. "We've been telling ourselves that hypothetically, a car costs Rs 1 lakh, and anyone who cannot afford that car is poor. We pour our expertise into trying to bring up the level of those people, but what if we just brought down the cost of that car to Rs 50,000? Half of all those people who couldn't afford it, now can, and are no longer poor." When he changed his view of poverty, he says, he was able to begin to make a difference. Poverty, he says, is not about tweaking people, and watching what they put their money into, i.e. "it is not about who is worthy to be 'The Poor', but what circumstances surrounding them make them poor, and how we can make the surroundings more affordable and purposeful to them."

Because we view these classifications very rigidly—your hunger is valid, but yours is not—a certain kind of shame is imposed upon some of those who go hungry. It comes from a certain kind of condescension from those who have never had to. It is as though all hunger is a result of either stupidity or not having tried hard enough. There is a devotion to the cause of one's own upliftment that is demanded of The Hungry: a devotion to a nutritionally-balanced calorie count, a squirrelling away of savings to meet the ends of hunger, nutrition, nourishment, a visible wanting to escape it and a parallel assumption that those whose choices leave them with hunger deserve no empathy. It becomes inconceivable that a hungry man may be driven by more than one cause or end, and that whether that end be aesthetics, beauty, self-pride, it is also his free will to choose. Instead, it is met with a value judgement, and faced with the sneer of the hand held out, the victim of hunger chooses to borrow where he can, or shut up and put up, rather than let it be known that he is hungry. This in itself becomes an incentive to stay in or acquire more debt.

This is the flaw of a lens that evaluates all problems with how much money is generated by or thrown at it and creates power structures out of those as well. Debt is as much a power structure — good debt, constructive debt, debt that contributes to the economy, boosts education, spurs spending versus needless debt, selfish debt, and unthinking debt — as wealth. The top percentile of India's wealthy also has the most debt. But their debt comes from financial institutions, and is a symbol of not just their own prosperity, but their contribution to the boom of the economy. Many of those who spend are borrowing from their own future, and from the buoyancy of the economy around them. Is debt that contributes to experiential knowledge and gain — networking because of a coffee you can't afford — good or bad compared to debt that acquires material objects whose value depreciates? Who decides whose debt is which category? Rather than a judgement on the people, the taker of debt, the critical eye needs to extend to the circumstances that make that debt possible and required.

As George Orwell puts it in *Down and Out in Paris and London*: "Why are beggars despised? — for they are despised, universally. I believe it is for the simple reason that they fail to earn a decent living. In practice nobody cares whether work is useful or useless, productive or parasitic; the sole thing demanded is that it shall be profitable. In all the modern talk about energy, efficiency, social service and the rest of it, what meaning is there except 'Get money, get it legally, and get a lot of it'? Money has become the grand test of virtue. By this test beggars fail, and for this they are despised. If one could earn even ten pounds a week at begging, it would become a respectable profession immediately. A beggar, looked at realistically, is simply a businessman, getting his living, like other businessmen, in the way that comes to hand. He has not, more than most modern people, sold his honour; he has merely made the mistake of choosing a trade at which it is impossible to grow rich."

"We lived on glucose biscuits for a few months"

Aakarsh Prasad, 29, BITS Pilani graduate, New Delhi

In hindsight, being broke always seems funny. It's just not so when you're actually living it. Delhi is a cheaper city to live in than Mumbai. You can still get food for Rs 15 — a kulcha, chhole, a parantha — it's solid food. In Mumbai, where I lived for a year and a half after I graduated, you can only get vada pav or pav bhaji, which you can't really eat every day. It's very easy for people to say, 'just don't go out, don't join the team and pay that Rs 1,000-2,000 lunch or drinks bill'. But you have to also understand that when you are new to a city, you also go to work to meet people — they are the only people you know. If I don't join in, I have no one to talk to all week. So, isolation from work coffees or lunches pretty much means complete social isolation. It also does affect your image in the workplace. You get labelled an oddball, a loner, unfriendly, not a team player. Human Resources is watching all of this. How you get along with your colleagues is noticed and remarked upon. I think corporates and metros are a bad mix. Networking is important to move up in life. They are the guys who will push your resumes when you are looking for your next job. You can't say you don't need people unless you're the next Steve Jobs. I was better off than most people who came new to their jobs — I'd been in a boarding school since the fourth standard, and so I knew how to live on my own, I wasn't overwhelmed, but even I got stuck in debt. It's something you have to learn. The first few months, you're just making mistakes and figuring it out, but that's enough to suck you in, because it's a loop. One hit and you're gone. Four of us once went drinking and ended up with a bill of Rs 35,000 at a bar. Obviously we didn't have the money to pay for it, and we were too drunk to do anything about it then, so we left our cellphones at the bar and promised to come back the next day. The next day, we borrowed from various friends, paid the bill and retrieved our cellphones. But it's a cycle. That means you've already spent Rs 10,000 of next month's salary, which means you're going to have to borrow again to make ends meet. It's infinite. For a while, we survived on Sodexo coupons that one of us got, but it was two months of Parle G packets and bananas after that. You can't tell your parents about issues like this.

When I first moved to Mumbai I tried to take the train. But I just couldn't do it. It was too frantic, like we're all animals. This is no way to live, I thought. So I began to take the cab. I still do, Rs 400 a day for the 12 km stretch to work. Then everyone goes to parties where you've to spend on alcohol and drugs and pot. There are customary gatherings. Each and every lunch is split amongst five people and you do end up paying quite a bit. If, like me, you head a team, then it's on you to take them out now and then to boost morale. We are all trying to be part of this capitalist economy. Three of us guys now share a three-bedroom apartment in Gurgaon. I earn Rs 50,000 now and we pay rent of Rs 45,000. We are all broke by the 15th or the 20th. You see your salary going out in batches. Rent, then groceries, then some utility bills like phone and electricity, commuting and then you're done. I do not shop for clothes, I have no impulse buys, I'm not eating fancy stuff, I don't drink during the week, only the weekend, and we have a kitchen but we don't *know how to cook anything beyond an omelette or a sandwich, so we order. Also, metros don't like to give homes on rent to bachelors, so that hikes the rates up every few months. That's also destabilising. I think people who work in the city that they live in, living at home with parents, having their bills taken care of, don't realise how socially destabilising it all is. How important something as basic as food is to how you wake up and feel every single day. You have to engage with the system the way it presents itself to you. If you don't, you're not a part of it. You will never grow within it. You may as well give up and go back to your village now.*

The Homeless

To Be Without A Home, Like A Complete Unknown, Like A Rolling Stone Bob Dylan

"Because society believes 25-year-olds can change the world"

Ronnie Kuriakose, 26, Publishing Publicist, New Delhi, from Kochi

I had gone overseas to do my Masters degree and when I came back, I left Kochi, Kerala to join a major publishing firm in New Delhi. I started as an intern and worked my way up and am now a publicist. I've lived in New Delhi for over two and a half years. I live in Nizamuddin now. On the side, I design card and board games and plan to start my own company with a couple of friends — we're almost there.

Coming to New Delhi from Kochi I had to adjust a lot, Delhi is huge and it is hard to connect. Over here, if you work in a good place, you have to maintain the mask of doing okay. Especially for someone like me who has two sides to my work personality. I do a lot of events, have done several with the Vice President of our company, but I'm also the down to earth guy who will shake hands with the security guard. So my ease of access to both the top tier and the bottom tier is important to who I am and how I am perceived in my professional role. I am always well dressed. My look and feel is of a polished, dapper guy.

When I came, I was new, and I didn't know anyone except the people I worked with and I couldn't bother them. In November 2014, I didn't have a proper place to stay, and when my lease expired, I didn't have enough money to get a new house in my budget. So I had to rent a shabby room in INA, New Delhi. It was the only place I could get a room for Rs 1,500 a month. It was shabby, to say the least. There have been days when I would live on a single meal a day and still show up completely dapper in my suit, at events I had to organise and host.

These are the two sides of the personality coin. While trying to save as much, if you have committed to a certain lifestyle, you have to spend. There is no choice. If you have to host client meetings, you have to take them to a proper social club – I met Subramanian Swamy last week – I can't go to a cheap joint. Recently, an author asked me how he should sign his books, so I've been undertaking independent research to ask design firms the best font, colour, what should it say, how best authors should sign books. I take up personal projects as part of my professional act because I invest in making myself a better professional.

I live near the Golf Course now, so I called up and asked if I could volunteer. Every Sunday I wake up at 6 AM and head to the Course; while I volunteer I meet people I would never get to know in other circumstances. I also tag along to go to the Race Club, or the Gymkhana. These are places and people I would not encounter otherwise.

Today, it is a necessity to do such things.

Part of it is because of the added pressure on anyone my age by the rest of the world. The world believes millennials can change the world. Because I'm 26, I'm expected to know. If I don't come up with ideas often, there are people younger than me – 20-year-olds are tech savvy and knowledgeable and their learning is rapid – and those older than me, whose expectations I must meet. This dual competitiveness requires it.

At first I thought it was just me, but then I look around and realise everyone is going through this silently. Many contemplate depression and suicide, because cutting back on resources, no food, no socialising, leaves them desperately lonely. They just don't say it because it will spoil their image. I can't blame technology alone but this very real lack of companionship has something to do with it. We are all isolated now.

♦ ♦ ♦

A new kind of homelessness

Two kinds of homelessness are imposed by the pressures of the new age on migrant urban white collar workers in cities: first, a material lack of affordable housing, and the second, a notional loss of the idea of home. Both contribute to a sense of being impoverished.

The material loss of home

Sixty-nine per cent of the Indian population is now in the prime house buying age of 20-40 years according to a Bloomberg report in April 2017. Increased migration, the poor infrastructure, a builder focus on luxury housing, and government focus on rural housing, was leading to urban shortages. The recent real estate market reforms under the Housing for All programme are aimed at making a difference. There is hope that the market slump will turn around towards a $1.3 trillion push. For now, the reality on the ground is harsh. The luckless, light-pocketed, roving budget renter remains at the mercy of landlords' whims till the much-needed changes come into effect.

The Jones Lang LaSalle's (JLL) report, 'Affordable Housing in India', points to severe shortages in the housing market. With steadily increasing urbanisation, not only signifying an alarming rise in the concentration of people, comes an implicit competition for not just housing, but the amenities that support that life, from water and sanitation to public transport and access to public spaces. Private development in India, however, largely targets higher income housing, with premiums for developers. According to MHUPA (Ministry of Housing and Urban Poverty Alleviation) norms, the Middle Income Group needs 1,200 square feet at EMIs not exceeding 40 per cent of the monthly income to qualify as having affordable housing. It's safe to say pretty much no one without an exorbitant luck factor in that tax bracket in India, certainly not in Mumbai, has even half of that space to himself, even with rentals, forget purchase.

Even as the prior community support structure crumbles, what it is being replaced by is the 'shared economy'. The shared economy bypasses not only the cost of investment in an asset but also the cost of maintaining it. Housing is a major area where the shared economy functions to substitute ownership. Start-ups like Restaway, RentalUncle, NoBroker, etc. cater to this crowd. The average rookie employee shares a home that size with three to four other room- or house-mates. Most just get by and take what space they get. Data on this demographic is slow to accumulate but companies like Nestaway, which has received $43.3 million funding already, projects a listing of two lakh unique properties by end 2018 and is aiming for a prize chunk of India's $10 billion 10 million-user heavy rental property pie. NoBroker, with a 1.5 million customer base across four cities, is an over $20 million company today.

As whimsical landlords and brokers raise rents year on year, some because they take objection to meat eating, alcohol, partying, late nights, boisterousness, or even religion—all the prerogatives of exploratory youth—they force the young to live in the expectation of shifting repeatedly, like nomads. As rents rise, the disposable income drops. According to JLL, the higher the income the greater the proportion of the drop: "If house rents increase from 15 per cent to 20 per cent, the disposable income for a Lower Income Group household (person with a monthly income of Rs 10,000), reduces 30 to 35 per cent. Whereas for a person with monthly income of around Rs 1,20,000, it can be seen that when rent increases from 15 per cent to 20 per cent, the corresponding reduction in surplus income is from 64 per cent to 59 per cent", the report states.

Affordability, then, becomes not an absolute, solved magically with the next pay raise, but is a problematic proportion of what must be spent of any income in order to be able to afford to keep earning it. Factors like class, status, hierarchy of influence, apart from various social factors, affect the address one chooses to stay in.

Housing, thus, bears the ability to become unaffordable across income groups.

The lens of who needs affordable housing is, and rightly so, focussed on the 88 per cent who lack access to civilised and comprehensive housing solutions, but it also then overlooks and allows to hide the poverty-in-plain-sight of the uncounted many who also need some systemic redressal. Some of those lost in this statistical gap are the ones stranded between solutions they can't afford and systems, social and economic, that fail them.

As the city changes from, as Mumbai-based architect Kamu Iyer puts it, "neighbourhoods of community to neighbourhoods of affluence", i.e. how much one earns that now determines which areas one may live in, as opposed to the old neighbourhoods of India that were based on community and kinship, the aspiration to physical addresses become prime tools to rise up the ranks.

A city is never just buildings. In reconfiguring the city to render some parts of it more exclusive than others, we have ensured that some people who live there are perceived as more valuable than others. And those who are left out, as it is inevitable some will be, must find other items of value to supplement their image.

The notional loss of home

"All you who sleep tonight, far from the ones you love, No hand to left or right, and emptiness above. Know that you aren't alone, the whole world shares your tears, Some for two nights or one, Some for all their years", wrote poet and novelist Vikram Seth. It could well be the anthem of those seeking shelter under the promise of a new urban landscape.

Left without money to pay exorbitant rents, renew leases, or afford the basic privacy of personal spaces like a bathroom or a cupboard or a sleeping space with a door that locks on it, without trappings like television or refrigerator, and quiet spaces within the home in which to relax or be, the unmoored young are turning to coping with this culture shock in ways that work for them.

For many, the escape comes by finding ways to stay out of the place of dwelling. This is achieved by either finding entertainment that will keep them outdoors for considerable lengths of time—partying into the wee hours, going out for dinner or a movie, parking themselves at coffee shops, using alcohol or drugs, finding 'home' in friendships and the more bearable homes of other friends, in the arms of transient lovers to make the space hopping more exciting and palatable, and for some, by pulling over time such that they work late into the night, take a cab home and crash. Several speak of the immense loneliness of being cramped into what makes for affordable urban dwellings. All these escapes cost money, energy, time, and an investment in a certain image building. Access to night clubs, restaurants, alcohol, the sustenance of specific kinds of groups of friends that keep this lifestyle afloat, and the apparel that suits the lifestyle, all require some amount of monetary investment in the process. In the overcrowded rooms full of the lonely young, the clique, therefore, begins to gain paramount importance.

But how prevalent is it? In an informal online survey, several young people spoke of being rendered homeless, whether for one night or more, in India's major metros. Forty three per cent had never been in that situation. Nineteen per cent were homeless for one night only, 21 per cent for multiple nights at a stretch, and 9 per cent for several weeks. Four per cent had faced it for months on end. Of these, most had either been tossed out by landlords fed up of waiting for their dues, or just didn't have the money to renew leases or find new flats. Seventy five per cent resolved it by staying with a friend or relative, some found a room in a cheap lodge or hotel. Three per cent slept at their workplace after everyone had left while pretending to work late hours. Three per cent slept in their car, while 14 per cent slept in a public space like a bus stop, which gave them access to rest rooms. One person said he'd slept on the pavement. Eight per cent of respondents said they'd used dating apps at some point to split the cost of a hotel room with a temporary partner, and three per cent said they were currently using dating apps to find partners that would help them have a new place to stay every night. As an indicator of a much larger malaise about which little data is available, the figures speak to a small minority faced with having to take extreme measures to cope.

"They either obsessively save or obsessively spend. There is no balance."

Ramya Ravi, 25, works in a tech start-up, Mumbai

We live in India, but want to live like Americans. The idea of what a successful group of peers looks like was set by the sitcom F.R.I.E.N.D.S. that our generation grew up on. That's the mental image we have of what a working, functional, urbane peer group looks like – sitting in a coffee shop sipping those coffees. That's what we are all trying to be. I came to Mumbai to work in 2013 and moved to Powai, where I worked. Today, everyone who comes in from out of town finds neighbourhoods according to their occupation. The start-up crowd lives in Malad and Powai, the film crowd in Versova, the advertising crowd in Bandra, the financial crowd in Worli, etc. So once you are home, you are able to subsist in your own little bubble.

Home to work, that was it, I never ventured beyond, so in that sense you could say I lived in my oasis. I walked to work. It was its own mini ecosystem. In the start-up world, you will find that many people come from the same kind of background – middle class, salaried, working their way up. So many CEOs don't live on profit-sharing models; they can't. They want a salary to take home at the end of the month. Because everyone has bills to pay. Many have come from small towns like Bhilai and struggled through IITs and they don't get jobs right away. Many continue to stay in the IIT hostels till they stabilise. Or they share rooms and support each other; that way the IIT graduate and start-up circuit is very helpful.

So why do they spend recklessly? When they start earning, they've lived badly for so long, worked so hard, they start spending. Rents in the Powai area are fairly high and most cope by sharing rents. They aspire to buy cars and bikes. The most common dream is to buy an Enfield or a Harley Davidson. Then there are flat screen TVs and air conditioners and music systems on EMIs. There's also pressure from society to get married, settle down, seem successful. No woman looking for a prospective groom today wants to honeymoon in an Indian destination any more. That's just not an option. Many of them complete their education with student loans of about Rs 5 to 7 lakh at the IIT level. If they go higher, into the IIM or ISB level, it can be Rs 15 lakh. Some have gone overseas on their final year projects, so they have the exposure, they see that life, and they know what we live without. So they want it. They either obsessively save or obsessively spend. There is no balance. Founders are typically more responsible because they are answerable to venture capitalists, so systems of checks and balances are in place. You won't find them cheating on taxes or that sort of thing. Eighty per cent of those working here live without their parents. Some share up to four in a house, others two. Many are from lower middle class families from small towns, so the ability to support and save is ingrained in them.

Most begin on salaries of Rs 6-8 lakh and they aim to jump high. They want 40 per cent hikes. Living in hostels with pocket money and bus pass, most don't know how to manage their money. They have no financial planning because they have been cosseted and never lived away from home. I worked in an ad agency and had friends who earned Rs 15,000 and took Rs 20,000 from their parents — they were taking more in support than they were earning in order to stay in the job. In the start-up world, you can wear superhero t-shirts and jeans. In other jobs, your clothes matter.

We are also creating a society geared towards spending now. The money you earn and the money you spend matters. Sometimes, I visit relatives and find cousins as young as in the sixth standard discussing upgrading their cellphones or their Playstations. They are handed everything on a platter. For many of us, we have never *seen our parents use credit cards and so we don't know how best to use it now. But what you teach the young is what they take forward in terms of spending. What they don't know they can't navigate. Parents obviously cannot teach their children everything, but they can certainly empower their children to think every decision through. But by micromanaging every decision – from the smallest to the biggest – when many leave home for the first time, they are handicapped in the decision-making space.*

♦♦♦

The inability to navigate this new urban homelessness also has a seemingly unrelated domino effect: the exaggerated demand for student housing. From the Film & Television Institute of India, Pune, to the Jawaharlal Nehru University (JNU) campus, New Delhi, to IIT Mumbai and state universities, the dormitory rooms of hostels in our educational institutions are full of students who may have earned their fancy degrees but cannot, until they earn their first couple of salaries, afford to put down a deposit and pay brokerage in order to start a completely independent earning life. In 2016, students of Delhi University pitched tents in front of the administrative block to highlight the lack of affordable accommodation. Students who have access continue to live in hostels long after they have graduated, which creates problems in major educational institutions. Many who graduate from IIT Mumbai secretly continue to bunk with juniors, in exchange for the promise of inducting them into their success when the start-up they join or found begins to pay them sufficiently. Accommodation is bought and sold and rented on this dream in areas like Powai, just outside the IIT in Mumbai and in start-up incubating areas like Electronic City in Bengaluru.

Makarand Paranjape, Professor of English at JNU says the problem arises because subsidised housing makes it incredibly affordable. Room rent of Rs 20 a month, zero payments for utilities, subsidised food at about Rs 1,600 a month (three meals, two teas)... "It's the cheapest place to stay in South Delhi, whether you have a job or not, whether you have finished your degree or are still studying." It is equally reflective of the gap between the expectations set up by our education system, and the reality of what a fresher may start earning and expect to live on once a graduate. Students often lack an alternative to extending their student status. Outside the cocoon of the campus, is a harder life the students are ill prepared to face, one where the bills will be due.

A few young people confess to having struck up or stayed in sexual relationships for the convenience of cheap or shared housing options, in the understanding that the relationship, like the lease, comes with an expiry date.

Urban uprootedness also has a domino impact on consumer behaviour. In such a sustained unmooring of a living environment, the spend, what one is able to tether oneself to, acquires importance. As one young woman put it: "When you share your life with four strangers, at your work place you are the minion, you have left home and so back there they think you're doing okay and you can't let them know otherwise, and on some days I don't have food to eat, what do I have but one cellphone and the ability to dress up or have fun sometimes? Must everything be a punishment?" What one has the ability to own, when one has the ability to own very little, becomes key. These may be notional: a holiday, clothes, gadgets that afford private conversations and space, from smartphones to headphones, and access to elite spaces, wherein space is at a premium, become worth the money, whether one can afford them or not.

By segregating housing on economic lines rather than community lines, society has effectively hung placards around people's necks that mark them out according to their hierarchies of income as opposed to the last two decades of migratory patterning that saw localities formed on the basis of community and language. To counter or fit in with this ecosystem, one of two things occur: young people are cramming themselves into shared apartments in expensive localities, or they are tethering themselves to rental housing start-ups to find the cheapest houses in the most expensive localities. For those who can't do either of these things, visible status symbols come to compensate. The differentiator becomes what one can individually own to set oneself apart from the peer group, or that sets one within a higher income peer group. This could be in the form of a smartphone, or a watch, shoes, or the kinds of clothes one wears, or the car one drives. The brand becomes all the more important to create a statement that counters where and how one lives.

The city itself reconfigures itself to 'neighbourhoods of affluence', and young people, immensely conscious of how they are defined by how much they are seen to make, rush to reallocate themselves to the class hierarchies that that reconfiguration creates.

"We network where we live"

Neyha Moindra, Advertising Executive, Bandra, Mumbai

I have lived in Mumbai for nine years and this is the sixth house that I'll be changing in September. Till now I've had flatmates so now I'm relieved to be renting a studio apartment all by myself. It's very different to live with other people, especially when you come from a small town and have never had to live like that before. It's a huge, huge culture shock. For the first two to three years, I lived in a paying guest apartment. We were four girls, sharing two to a room. Then it was an apartment with five people. Then a one-bedroom apartment with another girl. When you live in that kind of proximity to people you have to mould your lifestyle around theirs. It took one year for me to adjust to life in the city. After graduation, I didn't want to live in a hostel, you have to make compromises. You need the freedom to explore a city. The idea of living with people is great, but it's not so great when you are adjusting but others aren't. You try to make peace, but it's difficult. People have different temperaments. You also make the choice to buy into a specific urban lifestyle. It comes at a cost. What you pay for it to make yourself more comfortable, or how little you pay and stay mentally stressed. I'm paying a ridiculous amount of Rs 33,000, which is more than half my salary, to live in Bandra. It's prime area and I love it here. I feel safe. I find the culture freeing, convenient and secure. My work commute is done in 35 minutes. I don't have a circle of friends outside. I do see it as an investment in myself, in the advertising and film industry network. You can go down to any café and be inducted into a social-plus-professional circuit. If you lived elsewhere, you'd miss out on all that.

♦♦♦

The romance of the roofless

The film industry has had lots of, what it likes to call, 'struggler' stories of everyone from lyricist Javed Akhtar to actor Shah Rukh Khan to actress Sarika sleeping in public spaces, on the pavement, or in cars in the interim before they made it big. But even up to three decades ago, when these stories last originated in pre-liberalised India, was a time when such risks were the fantasy—to find fame and fortune in a Dick Whittington's London cityscape where the pavements are paved with gold. The seeker was the exception, the disruptor, the tentative dreamer, and not the norm. In the new cityscape, there is less illusion about how easily success comes, but the hierarchy of affluence determines who the strugglers are, and they now come from every field, not just film.

He with the stone pavement for a pillow in an unfamiliar city, however, remains as dramatic a tipping point to the rags-to-riches story as any cinematic trope.

When Anurag Kashyap thinks of his days of struggle in Mumbai, it's the finding a place to stay that bothered him the most. Influenced by Vittorio di Sica's film *Bicycle Thieves*, Kashyap, who was then with the Jana Natya Manch theatre group, decided he had to make it to Mumbai in order to make it in life. He relocated with Rs 5,000 in his pocket. Arriving in the city with very little idea of what the actual cost of living and finding work here involved, he soon found himself sleeping on the streets, in the terraces of buildings, and on the beaches of Mumbai. A friend found accommodation in the St Xavier's College boys' hostel, which meant sneaking in through a window and three illegal entrants sleeping on the floor of the hostel room at night. In the meanwhile, Anurag found work at Prithvi Theatre, until he began scripting for films and television serials. Today the influx of the struggler has extended beyond Bollywood to sectors like media, advertising, tech, BPOs, and financial services, to new age industries, from animation and editing to fashion, and that ubiquitous be-all do-all term, 'consultancy' work. All believe that some struggle is an inherent part of the process.

Thanks to the magic of cinema, however, despite the discomfort required in order to be productive while crammed into living rooms like sardines in a tin, there is a glow to the whole exercise that makes the sufferers believe it is a much-needed sacrifice for times to come.

₹3.

The Driven

**Oh Lord, Won't You Buy Me A Mercedes Benz?
My Friends All Drive Porsches,
I Must Make Amends.** Janis Joplin

"This commute seems so savage"

Radhika Sengupta, 29, Advertising Executive, Mumbai

We have become this do-it-yourself generation post 2007. We are taught in India that in order to achieve anything good, we must struggle. So when the struggle comes, we assume that this is how it must be, and do it. If you do not get through it, you don't deserve the success that comes after. To feel means that somehow your ma raised you wrong.

Those of us who came to Mumbai from small towns, the only trains we have seen in life are long distance trains that we took on holidays with families and packed lunches. We don't know how to commute like this. It is exhausting. It seems so savage, there is nothing civilised about it. We come from towns where we walked or cycled to school. We grew up in small social circuits. So we begin to think that if I am earning enough, the least I can do for myself is to at least show up to work in a civilised manner. It may seem like fake pride, but also remember that in small towns, the most brilliant ones went to the cities. You reach here and you realise that you are just one among so many. And the world is a very vicious place.

◆ ◆ ◆

Socialist India's biggest dream was to one day be stable enough to own one's own home, spawning an entire housing-loan generation. A post-liberalised India began to value instability, and eschew putting down roots. In the new age, the ability to adapt, be absorbed across multiple functions, and be mobile, whether you are the pizza-delivery guy, whizz-kid coder, or the CEO of an MNC, are far more important skills than a vow to never abandon your post. Within a couple of generations, the equations of what constitutes success have moved from standing still to being quick on your feet.

In that environment, the house becomes too expensive an investment, not just in monetary terms, but also in terms of its inability to offer the right brand-value and neighbourhood-of-affluence bracket that would make it attractive to a young person, besides being redundant as it clashes with the need for mobility. The car, thus, becomes the substitute house. Young people just out of college are no longer thinking how to save and buy a stable home, but which major metros of the country and the world they can possibly gain work experience in. "What one has the ability to experience becomes far more potent a phrase than merely the showing off of one's means — fewer people want to own a well-known, expensive brand for the sake of it, and more for what it says about what kind of lives they seem to lead — and what young people are spending on is the ability to buy that experience," says Karan Chauhan, International Marketing Manager for Bullet Enfield. The car is not only as big an investment as a house once was, with its customisable exteriors and interiors, it is also a pretty loud statement for its owner. "Get into any young person's car and you will find it intensely personalised, from the kind of music console, to the dashboard to the number plate, and with it crammed with everything that person needs within hand's reach — whether that's make-up and an extra pair of party clothes or heels under the seat, or music, a power bank, gadgets ... the car is literally a mobile mini home for a young person today."

Why would a young person spend anywhere between Rs 5 to 25 lakh or more on a vehicle? Essentially, it also becomes a vehicle for the personality of its owner. It speaks to his experience of life and his career. It is also a worthy investment for that reason because it is *not* a long-term investment. Unlike a generation prior, in the 1990s, when a car was bought after much deliberation and was bought *for* its longevity, a commuter vehicle that served a family functionally, today's models are bought *to* be upgraded in a couple of years' time, allowing room for the flexibility of the owner's personality. In expressing the opposite of stability, the vehicle also capitulates the occupational mobility of its owner. The individual today is not stuck in a dead-end job because he has EMIs to pay. He is a module in himself, capable of being a consultant. Should he quit and decide to take his career off road, the investment in a car, SUV or bike goes with him, allowing him also to consider it a viable boost to career options that allow him to freelance, whether in mountaineering, tours and travel, photography, organic farming or in a start-up creating customised delivery services via an app—the promise of mobility extends the owner into a wide range of viable options for profitability. The car, thus, becomes an extension of the brand of the individual in more ways than one.

It is a change that has come from selling culture in a certain way according to Chauhan. Modern television and movies sell this lifestyle. The visual media of the pre-1990s didn't. "A sense of security meant a very different thing for someone in pre-liberalised India and means a very different thing to a young person today. When a young person today says he has a sense of security, he means he is ensconced in the lifestyle that he wants for himself, and has the freedom to go do something else tomorrow. That is security for him. The gamble on freedom. Because he is not afraid of his tomorrow, he is brave. He is not afraid of spending money, because to him his tomorrow is assured, and it is assured not on the basis of some employer who will guarantee him a salary, but on the basis of his own ability to find and do work. I find this generation very ready and willing to do anything. The earlier generation was very rational about their options. To earn meant there were fixed things you had to do. For this generation, rationalisation takes a back seat. Nothing is off limits. Therefore, today, if earning is open, spending also happens much faster. It's all on the spur because its not long term, because gambles are welcome, because what is bought depreciates and can be sold off as a tax write-off, and everyone is always open to change. There is no time between thinking and happening, the young are very confident. Nobody wants to live their grandfather's dream. They want what's reachable, and they want instant gratification."

"The first thing I bought was a car"

Deepika Padukone, 30, Actress

When I first moved to Mumbai, the first thing I bought myself when I had money was a car. I had late night shoots, had to travel to auditions, and had to wear outfits that I didn't feel good taking a rickshaw or a cab in. I had to go half way across town. Commuting in Mumbai is stressful. Also, when you have to attend these events and things, you have to show up looking half decent, and that involves carrying make-up, or accessories, or shoes and I would have no place to put them. But also, I was working so hard that I needed to sleep. So the time I spent commuting became the time I could just put my head down and sleep for a bit. The house was less essential. You could rent. But the car was what gave you a sense of security in this city that's constantly on the move, that you could keep up, and do your job, and function on the go.

"If I had changed my car, would my career have grown faster?"

Kalki Koechlin, 32, Actress, Mumbai

I've grown up in a different way. I've never had to run away or deal with emotional pressure. Ever since I've been in the industry I've been driving a Maruti Swift. It's a small, useful car. But it's not a 'badi gaadi'. Directors often ask me why I don't change it. It just doesn't interest me to change that. I've lived in a friend's house on the sofa. When I first came I lived in Mahim opposite the station. I would have to ride the train in these ridiculous outfits, the short, glittery dresses and make-up required for some role. People stare at you. I have always been a little bit willing for that to happen than borrow the money that I don't have. I do know that pressures exist. I still don't have a PR person, people keep telling me to get a stylist. But I don't see why I have to pay out Rs 50,000 to plant a story about my cat. I'd rather give that excess money if I had it to my maid and the people who actually run my house. I know of many struggles. A friend went to an audition and was told, 'you look like a gaonvaali'. They'll say it up front: 'What are you doing here?' 'Lose the thighs' 'Do something about your teeth' ... I knew there was five years left in my career when I turned 30. There are people who use Botox for laugh lines, girls way too young do it. It's an industry that requires a lot of maintenance – nails, spa and hair. Which neighbourhood you live in shouldn't matter either, Lokhandwala Andheri is cheaper than Bandra and what works for you should dictate where you choose to live. But it doesn't, and at the end of the day, I don't know if it helps that much. The right things will keep coming your way, but it is said that there is something in being seen. When you are in the limelight, attending parties and auditions are ways in which to get your next project–but it has never worked for me. I don't know how to advertise myself. I don't set up Google alerts about myself. I think one's work should speak for itself. But, yes, there are times when I wonder if I had changed my car, would my career have gone differently.

◆◆◆

The car as symbol of new age mobility
For a generation that grew up on the Hollywood trope of cars as 'Freedom Machines', there is no justification you can provide to getting into the Virar fast or the Delhi metro and standing way too close for comfort to others heading in the same direction. There is nothing differentiating about the process of the daily commute,

when all of modern life screams out from hoardings that the young individual must spend, from creams to educational degrees, to make himself stand out from the crowd. Cars, effectively mobile bubbles, become a mode of personal transport but also expression. In India, they are also mega status symbols, whether you can afford them or not, which is why Mercedez Benz finds its pre-owned car sales growing at 39 per cent per annum. Cars are, however, only part of a mobility ecosystem. In India, the other elements of that ecosystem that makes motion possible—roads, parking, access to fuel, the element of pollution generated, etc.—are government controlled or regulated and often, of inferior quality. The car here, again, shoulders the responsibility of the tug of the individual vs establishment and freedom vs social responsibility. In the 30 years since our roadways first had to physically expand to accommodate rising consumer traffic, the car, much like the smartphone—periodically changed by business communities at Diwali every year in India—has also become a symbol of change. It comes to symbolise a change of status, a change of employment, and an upgrade to financial stability. The car has come to symbolise independence and progress. From industrialist Gautam Singhania to cricketer MS Dhoni to actor Sushant Singh Rajput, all have aspired to be wealthy enough to buy cars, and then upgrade to super cars. "It's great to harbour a dream—people tell you it's bad, it's a vice, but it's not—the aspiration gives young people something to work towards", Singhania said, as he rolled out his super car parade. While India's penetration of personal cars may be much lower than other developed countries—China is the world's largest automotive market—the aspiration remains a mental poster tacked to the wall for many.

The Missing Istrivala

Nargis Chokshi, 27, Client Servicing Manager, Advertising Agency, Mumbai

"Why do you look so dishevelled? You have to meet clients. I expected better of you."

"Sorry Ma'am, I haven't been able to iron my clothes."
"Why? Is your istrivala on holiday or something?"
Tears rolled down her cheeks.
"For pete's sake, what's wrong?"
"I've been sleeping in my car, ma'am."
"Your car? Did something happen? Do you need help?"
"No ma'am, I bought it on EMIs using my first salary as down payment and then I couldn't pay my rent."
"So you gave up the house? Why not the car instead?"
"Yes. Because then everyone would know."

For those who cannot afford to buy a car, the option of the radio taxi, the Uber or the Ola, becomes a substitute. One that also drives their savings into the ground. It is akin to being driven home in a car with a driver, without having to bear the expense of running and maintaining one. In whichever way a young person in the 18-30 age group can, this is exercising his or her claim to the symbolism of the road. With the app-based cashless payment systems typically hooked up to an automated credit card payment, the 'buy now pay later' sequence creates the deception of it being a momentary status upgrade that comes temporarily free.

The state of public transport has much to do with how off-putting and offensive to one's self-pride a commute can be. A decade ago, Rutgers University's report on *The Crisis of Public Transport in India* identified several problem areas. Our public transport systems were slow, undependable, inconvenient, uncoordinated, and dangerous. There was reducing ownership of public transport services. The rise of urban sprawl without corresponding facilities means more trips, more often, for multiple purposes when you need things. There are very few self-contained townships in India, and very few public transport links between those that exist. A lack of government support through traffic prioritisation — the idea that you would reach faster and without much dent to your wallet if you took public transport—has been denuded. Those coming of age a decade later, in the now, inherit these problems as obstructions in real time.

Even so, buses carry 90 per cent of India's passengers, though in many cities it's a combination of minivans, rickshaws, and taxis. Railways carry less than a third of most cities' population, except in Mumbai, where 58 per cent of local commuter traffic uses the railways. Cities that use public transport the most are Kolkata, Mumbai, Chennai and New Delhi. The paradox of public transport in India is that services have to be kept at a minimal in terms of quality and cost to enable the lower and middle classes to benefit. If costs were raised, there is a fear these commuters would shift to private modes of transport. So while the ease of public transport exists, it is a begrudging one, and a status many aspire to move out of, not simply because it is crowded and exhausting, but precisely because it is inexpensive.

Why has the car come to be imbued with this burden of the status of mobility? Because it is the first step to outgrowing the choking, teeming homogenised mass that commutes. It is also for many, the first port of call of substantial self-ownership.

Most of those who come to Mumbai to find work claim that though the first thing they dream of purchasing is a house—tiring easily of shifting endlessly year after year or living on belligerent landlords' whims—the first thing one does buy or attempts to, is a car.

"If I can't own a house, at least let me own something!", says a young marketing and sales executive who lived for two weeks out of her car parked in various lanes in Bandra. The car seems to have offered her a sense of being in a safe space, in a locality she wanted to be in, while providing her the convenience of mobility, the sense of being in charge of he self and keeping her pride intact, at not having borrowed from others, no matter how broke she was. It's a different matter that when the petrol charges piled up on her credit card, maxing it out, she had to abandon that line of thinking, and the car, anyway.

"When you graduate from the IIMs, you think you owe yourself the good life"

Ashvin Kumar, 40, IIM-L Alumnus, Independent Consultant, Mumbai

I have been there many times. In 1990, as a 17 year old, I went for my National Defence Academy (NDA) selection to Mysore and Bangalore. I had little money with me, and the week's stay at Mysore extended for another ten days at Bangalore. First time out of a small town, in the glitter of a big city, my money was soon gone. After the medical evaluations finished and it was time to board the train back home, I had Rs 100 with me. I still remember that day. I bought a ticket for Rs 97 (cattle class, as some of our elected reps would call it), and bought a bunch of bananas for Rs 2. I still needed the Re 1 for the bus fare from the station. The bananas were soon over, and I managed with water for the next 30 odd hours, till I reached home.

Coming out of IIM Lucknow in 2000, I had already racked up enough outstanding in my 'free credit cards' given out by Standard Chartered, SBI and HSBC. Out of my salary of Rs 14,000 per month, Rs 5,000 were spent on repaying the education loan and the rest on rent, food, transport, card bills, etc. Luckily, I didn't have any friends in Coimbatore, where I was working then, so I managed to avoid the night outs. But when I went to Bangalore, the card balances got dialled back again, at Purple Haze and Night Watchman.

I managed to regain some lost ground and recover some semblance of balance, but lost it all in 2014 again, when with my salary of Rs 45 lakh per annum, against better advice, I got a luxury car under the company car programme at Rs 35 lakh. When you graduate from the IIMs, you think you owe yourself the good life and that tomorrow will come, and you will pay it off anyway. I sold my personal car, which was in excellent condition, lost Rs 5 lakh I had put in as down payment, and wrote off the Rs 1 lakh I had to pay additionally to close the car loan. I was laid off in 2015 and had to sell the company car, and shell out an extra Rs 7 lakh to settle its dues to get my relieving letter.

Financially, I am much better off today, but it still gives me nightmares thinking about what I had to go through in 2001 and 2002, when I had to lock my doors and sit at home, to avoid the collection agents who used to come banging on my door.

Have I learned? Maybe not. Probably a genetic defect. One thing I'm proud of so far: I haven't asked my family for money yet. I bought my first bike with the compensation I got from the Ministry of Defence (had to leave NDA after two years due to medical reasons). I bought a car, two houses, and survived two bouts of unemployment all without having had to ask my family to bail me out.

I'm more careful with money now, thanks to my wife, but it is not something that comes naturally to me.

The Boundary-less

Freedom's Just Another Word For Nothing Left To Lose Janis Joplin

"There is clearly a hunger prevalent"

Anjana Mehra, Director, Lakme Fashion Week, Mumbai

When I was a junior, modelling was a closed group of 10 to 20 lead models and we didn't go looking in small towns for talent. The respectability of modelling as a career was also questionable in small town India at the time. Today, it is a stepping stone to Bollywood and young men and women come from these same small towns full of ambition and ready to take the risks that will help them use this step up against all the competition. So it's more about prioritisation. In the glamour industry, 95 per cent of what you do is optics. Only 5 per cent is the discipline and drive. So, if aspirants prioritise looking good and being seen in the right places, sadly that is what an increasingly insensitive industry is beginning to demand now. At fashion weeks, I have heard of young models packing the food we provide, tucking them into their bags. We look the other way, but there is clearly a hunger prevalent.

More alarming, though, is that one hears of a loss of moral values — the exchange of sex for money. What changed it for Indian modelling aspirants are the market dynamics of the 1990s and 2000s when the Brazilians and the Columbians started flooding the market. International casting agencies began to take over the market. While there are those that are genuinely good and professional — they provide shared accommodation and take care of the visas and the meals of those they shoot with — there are other so-called agents and agencies that aim to place models with Bollywood, in modelling and into the party circuit. These are pretty much filled with women from Eastern European backgrounds. Local aspirants started to lose out on jobs because these entrants into the market were more willing to pose, to do the bikini shot, and to submit to the casting couch. Those who stuck to their moral values lost out while the rest became party whores.

A lot of the pressure is also self-created. If you have the strength of character and moral values, then you will sell based on the strength of your portfolio, your body and your ability to photograph well. When you walk into the modelling scene you have to know what you're walking into and what you are ready to walk out of. There is enough work out there for the talented. So you need to have your cut off, much as you would with gambling.

◆ ◆ ◆

It's called 'voluntary prostitution' now

In the office of the Police Commissioner of Mumbai, spokesperson Dhananjay Kulkarni says the police are keeping their hands off the party circuit, because what's going on has shifted to the sphere of the voluntary. Legally, the police knows young people everywhere are putting sex on the table in exchange for money, alcohol, drugs, gadgets like the latest iPhones, and expensive holidays or free meals, even places to stay, but won't and cannot do anything to stop it. Former Chief of Police and Chief of Mumbai's Anti-Terrorist Squad, Rakesh Maria says he's been screaming it from the rooftops for as long as anyone would listen to him. "Young people everywhere come to Mumbai on their own, and are drawn into a lifestyle beyond their comprehension. Their parents don't keep tabs on them, they have no relatives or elders or seniors who know what's going on in their lives, and they are exchanging sex for money, for alcohol, for gadgets, and drugs. These kids need their parents."

While Maria has been flogged for his sentiments on the subject, for getting all moral police, quite literally, about it, pub owners through the city tend to agree with the viewpoint. "Every day I see young people come to the bar and negotiate terms and be led away for exchanges they don't even realise have serious implications, forget on health, just on them psychologically", says the owner of a high-end Bandra pub. Every day, he says, young people line up with maxed out credit cards, over-order drinks, and stagger out completely inebriated with people they just met an hour prior. "Sometimes you overhear them negotiating and it's not a nice thing to witness, but we don't really intervene because it's mostly just an arrangement between two people." A prominent Santacruz politico and businessman says several young women, once sucked in, end up on an informal listing of 'available girls' that gets spread by word of mouth. "These are largely girls who are willing to go along with sex for the money, a list that gets passed around via Whatsapp," he says. Meeting points are as simple as messaging a car number on a specific road, into which women jump in after alighting from their rickshaws or cabs, and are taken to someone's home, or a nice hotel. "It's simpler for many of those seeking a night out because it's fresher—almost like dating, not like a sleazy hook up service. Most of the girls are working professionals, well educated, independent, English speaking and many businessmen are willing to fork out a little extra for that. It's nice to spend an evening with them; you can actually have a conversation. They are also very clear they don't want involvements, so it's not messy. It's just sex. It's just money. It's just a gadget."

Insiders in the pub and nightclub circuit say it's a short step from a free drink to the ubiquitous cocaine, and many of the drugs du jour that currently do the rounds. The overwhelming need to be in with a happening clique quickly becomes social currency that is all too easy for the vulnerable to be sucked into in the name of keeping up with the times.

The other side: Being propositioned

S Rajan, Australia-based NRI visiting India

In Dubai, a couple of months ago, I entered what I thought was an Indian restaurant for dinner. Turned out to be a 'club' playing Bollywood numbers and a lot of young ladies dancing on stage. Before I could leave, I was hustled to a seat by a smooth young pimp. On the other side, a heavy had me boxed in.

It was early, about 7ish, and there were no other customers about. He began the pitch and despite me repeating I was just after dinner, kept saying 'ek baar baat kar ke to dekho sir, aapko kaun pasand hai' (speak to her once and see sir, you might like someone) etc. In the end, just to get out of it, I spoke to one of them.

This girl was very well-spoken and groomed. She soon twigged I wasn't a mark and opened up a bit. Turned out to have just started working, the demographic you write about, on a 'two week vacation' with her friends. It also helped that there was no other prospects about I guess! Reading between the lines, this is apparently commonplace among the aspirational classes who want it all and now, especially battling the high rents and costs of urban India on a low salary.

The pimp returned and started offering deals. Just for some perspective, he began at 8,000 AED per night and dropped it to 6,000 AED before I put a firm stop to it. Even assuming the girls made 1,000 AED out of it, a ten-day effort could gross them about Rs 1.8 lakh. I can certainly see the temptation there for the aspiring.

I soon made my excuses and left. Now, I wouldn't be judging those forced in either through trafficking or true economic hardship, but this girl appeared to be in it for the bling which made me reflect on how materialism has overtaken some, hopefully not the majority.

While this trade is as old as the hills itself, this was my first 'live' encounter albeit accidental and left me more than a little saddened.

♦♦♦

A former mainstream beauty pageant contestant from four years ago who now dances at an underground nightclub in Santacruz says she got fed up trying to keep pace. "You spend a lot of money on hair and expensive clothes, getting dressed up and heading to red carpet events to impress people in the hope that you will get more work. The work doesn't come. You can't pay your bills. Men hit on you; you get offered money to do the same things that the world points out as hypocrisies. At some point, standing there, it seems so futile," she says, justifying her foray into dancing. "There is more honesty in this. I dance, I'm paid, I have bouncers for my security, and I'm not struggling any more. There is no one to impress."

"I traded sex till I bought my iPhone"

Shruti Sharma, 24, Mumbai

Yes, I have used sex to buy myself an iPhone. We live in an age of Tinder so I really don't think anyone is in a position to judge me. Single people, married people, straight people who are overtly gay, all kinds of people are having clandestine affairs and one night stands, so puhleez, spare me the moral judgement. I live in Versova in Mumbai and I work in IT in an MNC in Andheri East which hires a lot of young people like me for coding, web design and content. Almost the entire office is in the same age group so there is a lot of partying and hanging out we do together. Which means there are drinks flowing, and with all the taxes, even a split bill for drinks is a minimum of Rs 3,000. So yes, my starter salary in my first job is Rs 35,000 but I cannot actually live off it if I have to live at all. I am from West Bengal, and most of my friends here live with their families. I have rent and commuting costs because I am not used to these trains so I tend to take a cab or rickshaw from Versova to Andheri East whenever possible. So, obviously, what I can spend on is less than what I can afford. We have a canteen so that covers my food costs reasonably. I have never starved, but I cannot afford the costs of a good phone. One way we try to save money on drinking costs is attending house parties, sometimes of a friend of a friend and so on, so it's not always people we know directly. I was at a party once and someone asked if I'd sleep with him. People are quite upfront about these things these days and we were also a bit high. So I said 'Yes, will you pay me?' kind of jokingly, but he asked 'how much?' I didn't really know how much to ask because it was my first time exchanging money, so I just asked for Rs 5,000. I got it on the spot in cash out of his wallet. He put me on to a couple of his friends and I know you'll get judgey and all but these are all my kind of guys, the kind of men I would date if I met them randomly on a dating app, without really knowing them, so what's the big deal? Some of the men I've been with are still part of my extended social circuit. I see women putting out in return for a fancy dinner at a posh restaurant all the time, so I really don't catch the hypocrisy. And we used protection and everything. I bought my iPhone by the end of the month. Maybe it was the thrill of it. I don't do it for money now, but I do occasionally sleep with a guy if I like him in return for him paying for drinks and meals. I think it's empowering for me to own my sexuality but I also think it's important to know when to stop.

♦♦♦

What won't you sell to survive?

It is unfair of me to ask several to share their stories of being severely depleted without sharing my own. We've all been there, or almost, or have been pulled back from the brink. The domino effect of being broke at the start of your career and the loans piling up year on year is such that the savings never quite catch up. Payment milestones do. At first, it's a donation to a school, a term fee, one hospitalisation, or unexpected medical bill, one phone that died and had to be replaced out of turn, one unscheduled flight, and every accumulated rupee that you thought symbolised your recovery from insolvency and bad financial management has the potential to be wiped out. Then you're back to square one. And then you haven't had a vacation in over a year though you're working as hard as you ever have and have that mythical designation for seniority, which is clearly a sham in salary terms. I replaced my first credit card four years after I had given it up after my divorce. My mother was taking a bus to our home town, Kodaikanal, because the flight tickets were too expensive and my six-year-old son was travelling with her. It would have been a 19-hour journey sitting up, an impossible ask for both. The card returned, as did old ways. I soon took out a car loan. It all quickly piled up.

A year later, one of the most humiliating phone calls I ever made in my life was to the Hiranandani hospital, Powai. I had already sold my gold earrings, two bangles and the Philips DVD player to pay for lawyer's bills, holidays, credit card payments, and furniture, moving costs, school fees and clothes. This was before the age of cellphones when every time you upgraded you'd have another one lying around the house to dispose of for some sort of cashback. I had been meticulous about selling all my *raddi*, saving milk packets and old bottles to add to the pile. I was already living on subsidised rent in a flat owned by a friend and not had to put down a deposit or the brokerage. I had already lost all the friends I had borrowed from the last time and was ashamed of constantly having to ask my family for money. I was tired of the friends I had left constantly offering to pay for my share of dinners and drink with no real end to my status in sight. I'd do anything not to have to ask someone for money again. At my last visit to the gynaecologist, the doctor had, in the way that matronly old OB-GYNs do, commented that I was immensely fertile and it was such a waste that I was single. I was ovulating and was in perfect health and could have had a baby if I was married. So, I dialled the number that Google threw up and asked if I could get paid for donating my eggs. The receptionist took down my number, my name, my age, ascertained that I was a post graduate, below 30, and not insane, best she could on the phone, and then put me on hold while she called a doctor. The doctor, an older male voice who sounded mildly astonished at my brazenness, chided me. "You will have to have painful hormone injections every week", he warned. I was willing to risk it, I insisted. He spoke to me about implications on my health, my body, my psyche in a coaxing voice. Asked my motives. I told him I wanted the experience of motherhood without the responsibility. He spent over twenty minutes on the phone talking me down off the ledge. "Do you even realise the implications of giving your DNA?" he finally shouted down the receiver. Nervous, and running out of excuses, I cut the line. That was the closest I'd ever gotten to selling my body for cash. But it is also why I don't sit in judgement on those who do. I just got lucky because someone more responsible, a complete stranger, stepped in and took responsibility for my self-harm. If he hadn't, I'd be in several stages of regret today. Based entirely on my own experience of it, and gleaning from what several who've shared their very personal case studies tell me, what is that point at which you give up and veer towards the wrong decision? Pride. You can skip meals in private for days on end, or walk home for half an hour because you couldn't even afford a bus ride, as long as no one knows about it. At the precise point when the lack hits your pride and there is no solution in sight, does the debt become the trap, and you begin to feel hunted.

In as much as this book is a confession by many of that sense of wounded pride, it's also, in their candidness and insistence on using their real names (some names have been changed on request) and details of their intimate financial dealings and fall from grace, a breaking of the pattern. The refusal to live this lie, sit with a false sense of social achievement that in many ways society forces them to live up to. The fear of being unable to pay for drinks, dress a certain way, be seen at certain places, and be subsequently rewarded by the system for that behaviour. The insistence on being told and being seen is a lifting of the curtain of silence that surrounds it. This generation isn't as broke or bereft of courage and integrity as it looks.

"You never forget what it feels like to sell, not buy, gold"

Lisa Wagner, 24, Mumbai

There is a difference between those who are there to buy and those who are there to sell or exchange because they got bored of their jewellery, and those like me, who are shamefacedly there to sell because they need the money. You enter tentatively, you are convinced they're all watching you and you scan the room with a sinking heart. You are holding that one box with a bangle or an earring or a chain, that has meant so much to you, or seemed like the most expensive thing you could possibly own, only to find it is worth a few thousand, and will not only not cover the entire credit card pile up, but that you will have nothing – still in debt and no asset at the end of it. My word of advice is when you feel like buying something, first try to imagine what you own that you can sell for an equal amount as what you would pay to own the item. If you don't have that money coming out of anything you currently own, or can possibly get in the future, just don't buy it.

"We have to spend what time we have to survive"

Name Withheld, 28, Actress from Europe in Mumbai

I don't pay money I don't have, but this profession is insecure. I have spent money that I am earning on my face and body, on keeping fit and on teeth cleaning and straightening. If everyone else's teeth are straight and yours are not, it stands out. We are our own harshest critics; we like to correct ourselves before anyone else can correct us.

Actors are even more insecure than ordinary people. Our insecurities are being fed by the insecurity of everyone else, which is a false confidence. That is why they need to put you down to feel that for themselves. I do have a strong core but I will not lie, I have also not been as conscious of myself because I have been doing theatre since a young age, I have studied theatre in London and done theatre for 15 years, before working in India for six years. As an actor, you become more aware of how your body transitions. Yet even people who don't work in media are now in the same boat. Look around you – housewives, businessmen and women are all conscious of their looks. Even if the pressure wasn't coming to us from outside, it exists from the inside. I came to Mumbai with my then boyfriend, now husband, to give my acting career a shot. Europe is more systematic. That is great but it can be bad as well.

I am more proactive, so I sent out my bio data and followed up. I think it is my own lack of skill in doing this, else I would have got work faster. The industry is such that if you stay out of circulation for too long, they will stop calling you for work. You have to be seen, be visible. One year I had absolutely no work. It was a very tough year for me. I had cut my hair short that year. And this industry does not know how to project a white woman with short hair as an actor. When they hire a white woman, they don't want the quirky, they want the bombshell in a bikini. The roles are pretty stereotypical and it is hard to get anything substantial in size. It depends on the years you put in, the skill, and of course, luck. No matter how hardworking you are, first impressions are lasting. This is true of human nature. Showing up in a big car is important. If you are simple, it surprises them. They look at you as if you are an alien. In Europe, we are more practical. In Scandinavian countries, we are all egalitarian, even the Prime Minister would cycle to work, but here the segregation is so stark. It is very prevalent in all layers of society. If the producer won't comment on how you show up, your driver will. It is expected of you to be 'a class apart'.

In this scenario, I have learned that happiness can only come from within. We all know that, but we don't apply it. I try not to equate personal success with happiness. If you go down that path, no work is good enough, no performance is good enough. You have to know what you will not do. I do wish I had bigger breasts, but I am not going to go and get plastic surgery for it. Will it probably change my look, get me different kind of work, make me more money? Maybe, but it is scary for me. I will not sleep around and feel like shit to get ahead. I cannot handle it. I am not good at flattering people. If I'm trying to be pleasant to be absorbed, they will know. I am a terrible liar. Everybody knows the same success is not for everyone, but does not apply it. Sadly, wealth, money in your account, how many times you hit the cover of fashion magazines, that is what everybody sees, at the end of the day, nobody sees how happy you are or not. If a Deepika Padukone can battle depression with all her success, she was number one at the time and not necessarily happy, that goes to show, what pressure this industry makes you deal with.

I want a different kind of professional success, and I separate it from my personal happiness. But personal happiness will not give me the money to buy my own house. If I act in a play that gives me professional satisfaction, maybe 200 people will watch it. If I do an ad film that may cast me in a stereotypical role, 1.3 billion people will watch it. I have a friend, a director and ad film maker, who is so restless when he works. He is so successful, he has money, his ads are legendary, but he is always restless. Personal fulfilment is not there 100 per cent. We do not have time to be happy. We have to spend what time we have to survive.

SECTION II
Why We Spend

Expensive Degrees – Exploitative Workplaces – Easy Money – Evolving City

₹5.

Expensive Degrees

**Oh, I know our troubles will be gone, goin' gone
If we dream, dream, dream for free.** Patti Smith

"Life itself is debt"

Archana Pillai, Medical Student, SRM Medical College, Chennai

Where do you think people go in this country when they want an education? The assumption in this country is that everyone is corrupt, so everyone's parents must have money sitting in the cupboards. We don't. We have ambition however. So when we study our whole lives for that one admission which we have been told will change our lives — I am in medical but those who go through engineering face the same thing — and are hit with fees of Rs 21 lakh a year, those who can afford it take personal loans. So even before you have started earning, your parents are paying EMIs and you think 'Okay, once I start earning I will pay them back'. But you get there and realise the children of the rich have it easy. Those who are connected will get the jobs, the placements, the further degree overseas, etc. You are not eating or sleeping, are working extended hours, spending on nothing, walking around in shoddy clothes and trying to save by skipping meals, and some Johnny whose father made illegal crores is enjoying this so-called economic boom India is in. Then, your parents will save up to get you married. At some point, you throw your hands up and try to have a good time. One dinner, one movie, one dress, one earring and it'll all pile up. Then you tell yourself it's okay, what is this struggle worth if we have not lived? Anyway life is going to crush us. We will always *be behind everyone else. Don't worry. We get punished for momentary joy also. Life itself is debt.*

♦♦♦

The real cost of a degree

In one of my more inspired moments of wanting to quit journalism, quite fed up of perennially empty pockets, I walked into the Wigan & Leigh college campus, a private institute of higher education, to interview for a role as a professor of journalism. One of my primary reasons for being there, and not an institute like St Xavier's Institute of Communications, where I had studied, or Sophia's Polytechnic, the more prestigious of communications colleges, was this was a full-time course, and naturally, a friend who was teaching another subject there informed me, the payment to the teachers would be on the higher side. They had been advertising in the papers heavily and I had been told on good authority, they would 'snap me right up'. I remember sitting in the waiting room for my interview appointment as several students, most of them clearly well off, came in to take their admissions for the forthcoming year. Among them, was a young boy from Nagpur and his clearly lower middle-class father, unassumingly dressed in a crumpled checked shirt, their long-distance train-weathered suitcase dragged in and left by the door, a battered handbag by the side of it a complete eyesore in this posh reception area in Lower Parel. It was one of the last days to complete admission formalities, and they were evidently in a hurry. They had made it just in time. Sitting down on the chair closest to the receptionist, I saw the father's hand tremble slightly as he reached into his bag and pull out two cheques stapled to forms. He was old, he was exhausted, but mostly, his pathos emerged from his hope. That he was somehow buying his son a better future. I peered at the cheques. They were each of a couple of lakh—the total was way above anything my individual monthly salary had been to that date, over ten years in the business—and clearly the result of a bank loan, the cheques having been made out by HDFC bank as a banker's cheque.

I thought back to my own recruitment in the business, I had done a part-time course and had begun freelancing, and never had I been asked once, in my career, what degree I had and from where. I thought of all those kids who kept coming to newsrooms with stories and got printed just because they had a flair for language and research, and not because of their degrees. I looked at the boy, and, perhaps judgementally, believed he would not make it, because he hadn't a clue what he was getting into. At that point I wanted to reach out to him and his father and say, if he wanted to be a journalist, all he had to do was begin to write. At that point I realised if I took the job, I would be equally guilty of perpetrating the con myself: telling an entire generation that what they needed to succeed was an expensive degree and that acquiring this would polish off the inherent talent or lack of it, regardless, when I had been recruited and achieved my goals without any such. I got up and left the waiting room without waiting for my appointment that day. Journalism may pay less but it is a more honest profession than education, apparently. We are obliged to speak the truth to our readers. If I had had the courage to speak to the boy seeking admission that day, what I would have said is this: "Some of you will not make it, no matter how expensive your degree, so the least you can do is choose a profession where you will be happy".

As we systematise our education systems, we draw the first boundary that students must struggle to define their success within: 'You succeed if you are qualified to'.

Yet, we systematically fail to provide the ease by which to achieve this. Earlier in 2016, the IITs raised their tuition fee for undergraduate education to Rs 2 lakh per annum. IIM Ahmedabad now costs you Rs 19.5 lakh annually. These are the educational institutes at the pinnacle of higher education in India, and these are government-regulated fee structures. Government medical colleges like AIIMS come heavily subsidised and range between Rs 50,000 and a lakh. Private college fees range between Rs 10 lakh to 25 lakh per annum, with the cost of a full course ranging between Rs 50 lakh to Rs 80 lakh. The vocational or the alternative skills are devalued currency in today's educational systems.

The scene is not much easier for those who obtain grants and fellowships either. For many students, especially at the post-graduate level, says Professor Pushpa Trivedi at the IIT Bombay campus, problems kick in when their fellowship grants are delayed. "As it is these often only cover a tuition fee, and not living fees. Especially if one is from a disadvantaged section of society, you are forced to take personal loans or student loans. Many students begin life with debts in this way."

Apart from the fees is the fact that given the number of students applying to get in, seats cannot be got for love or money if you are not in the top percentile of either intelligence or wealth: 15 lakh students apply each year out of which just one-and-a-half lakh students actually get admission. The remaining eight-and-a-half lakh students have spent the last three years, if not more, studying—which often means expensive tuition classes, commutes, and physical and mental exertion—for disproportionate gain. Headlines focus on those who get in. Never on those who get left out. The result is a majority beginning an education already with the sense of having been short-changed by education, by opportunity, and by income. The same story repeats across sectors: nursing, medical, architecture, and legal. Pick the profession and a systemic void is created. The shortage of seats is estimated at 3 million a year. The lure is often the starting salary splashed across newspapers every year at campus recruitment time. 'Visa offered $115,000' and 'the highest pay package was Rs 93 lakh', etc. A steadily-rising fee structure and an acute shortage of seats has resulted in all kinds of parallel industries—from fake degrees to private educational institutions with no real credentials—mushrooming everywhere. And there are many willing takers, or desperate ones at any rate, willing to sell their souls to acquire a mark of being qualified to storm the professional world.

Narayan Ramaswamy, Partner, KMPG and education sector analyst believes that education costs are only going to go up in the near future with more and more players in the private education space. "There is no real way to put out an aggregate figure for student debt in India, but we can expect it to increase. We will see a hike in the cost of higher education in both private and state-run institutions. Within 20 years, the cost of tuition at an IIM has increased 20 times. That is a huge hike, and that's still government controlled. Obviously, the rate at an Indian School of Business is multiple times higher. Where once only a select few did a semester abroad, almost everyone does now. Costs go up because technology is not going to stay free for long. If we want good quality, access, faculty, etc. there is a cost to it. What will ease it out is the new focus on skill development. As more and more private sector foreign players enter skill development, you will see a turn in the quality of vocational education. That will expand not only educational seats, make more institutions available, but will stem the squeeze on many vying for a few at a very high cost, and limited returns."

With demand being greater than supply and private education offering solutions where the state fails, the fees come at a premium. Between 2013 and 2016, the number of education loans disbursed by Indian banks hit Rs 25,736 crores, distributed among 21.79 lakh students. Ninety-one per cent of the amount was disbursed by public sector banks. The total loan outstanding in education loans is Rs 61,831 crores as of March 31, 2016 as per RBI data.

Consequently, students today are coming into the professional world already laden two-fold: debt as well as a psychological sense of disadvantage of *already* being behind.

Throwing a student with these two disadvantages into a city full of consumerist lure that is advertised to prop up his self-confidence—from fairness creams to deodorants to nightclubs and brands of clothes and shoes that mark him out as *visibly* successful—is meat to a hungry lion. The disadvantage has, thus, been planted systemically and is filled systemically.

"To be honest, I broke up because it was just too expensive for me."

Sourya Subhanjan, Team Manager, Cognizant, from Odisha, working in Hyderabad

I just want to shut my machine at work, and go home and cry.

As team manager, you have to take your team out or go out with colleagues and both of those things cost money. It could be just one team lunch but it can set you back for the next two months. Then you get into a relationship. When you are on your own, it's okay to miss some movies or just stream things. I just broke up with my girlfriend because as lonely as I am without her, when you have a girlfriend, you have to go to the movies, where everything costs money—from tickets to the popcorn and Coke, and no boyfriend can ask his girl to pay. Then there are dinners and other small things that build up. Today, women also don't want to date a loser. They are very clear about wanting a certain standard of living, going out, having a good time. They earn, they are independent, and if you do not or cannot support even a couple of movies, dinners and shopping, then you are not worth it. You also want to do that for the person you are with. When you are not able to, you come to a point where you begin to question your role as a man. To be honest, I broke up because it was just too expensive for me.

This is apart from basic living expenses. It's only after moving to a place like this that I even knew what brands to buy, what is a basic brand of jeans that you should have—I've only just started wearing Levis. Until now I didn't even know that. I had never gone to a coffee shop, and didn't know what to order. People like me have never had Rs 200 coffees, but here this seems to be the thing to do. I left home, a very small town in Odisha, and find myself left with a great disconnect with my family, especially my father. They expect that once you leave, you will do well, earn money and then come home, marry someone they pick and settle down, and continue to follow all the conservative values that you had left behind. There is no language to explain to them that once you leave your small pond and see the world, your whole world-view changes. That who you are becomes different and that you are trying your best to balance both worlds. Also, I now see that so many practices they follow are wrong. It leads to clashes.

But these are the two worlds we are caught between. No matter how much I spend to fit in — buy the right brands, things which I learned only in the last year or two, and that become necessary to fit in, I am too fancy for my village and it is always too less for the world here. A small change is that when you work with tech, dealing with clients from all over the world, you lose your heavy native accent and you acquire an accent that becomes neutral. I have lost my childhood friends because of this — they think I have become too fancy. But I am still not seen as the articulate, cool speaker here.

For one I have gone too far, and for the other I have not gone far enough.

I slog hard every day and see those people get ahead who have the advantage of good upbringing, whose parents understand the value of brands, grooming, education and status symbols. They are the ones getting the projects in Australia and New York and Europe. I sit here and check Facebook every day and see their updates and posts about their great lives and wonder when my chance will come. If you login, you are left with this overwhelming depression of being left behind, if you don't login and socialise and mingle, or have a girlfriend, you are left with the complete isolation.

What is one to do? How is one to know?

♦♦♦

It's all very well to wax eloquent about having the pride, self-confidence and upbringing to resist peer pressure, but in reality, few who step into a room with a sense of disadvantage have the confidence to reject props that are tailored expressly to fill that void.

The marketing of this sort of image pushes students to buy what the economy needs to sell, and there is, thus, an insidious thrust on spending to succeed. Spend on education, and then spend to fill the void education leaves you with in order to fit in. Hand them loans, personal finance, make it too easy to have no excuse. And then tell them they're stupid for being in debt.

"He lives on raw tomatoes and bread"

Rohit Verma, Indian student in Germany

We are students in Dresden, Germany and there is this guy who is above 30. He is a Masters student from the Hindi hinterland and couldn't exactly ask his family for support. He works part time at the doner kebab shop as a cleaner, but he is only allowed to work 20 hours a week. So, after paying rent, there is very little left over. He lives on raw tomatoes and bread. That's the scariest thing I've ever seen. My senior told me not to compromise on food – that's the first thing students who travel overseas compromise on. After he finished his degree, he kept going from one university to another as he couldn't find a job. In the biting cold winters, his health was affected. It was scary to watch him. We use him as a cautionary tale now, to tell juniors not to compromise on food.

♦ ♦ ♦

₹6.

Exploitative Workplaces

But if you ask for a rise it's no surprise that they're giving none away Pink Floyd

"Upload the happy workplace to Instagram"

Shilpa Phadke, 27, Engineer, Thane

At team lunches, I sipped water. I drank soup. I ate only vegetarian starters. They would always pick the most expensive place, the hottest new place, the most fun place and I'd be counting literally what I was eating. But when the bill came, someone would breezily say, 'oh, I'll pay card and you all pay me by cash.' And I would be sitting there thinking, but come on, that's why I didn't eat, but you can't say that out loud when six other people are not complaining. People just assume you're not well, or didn't feel like eating. It won't strike them that you don't choose to spend at that time. And it's not about having the money. When you don't, it's worse, but even if I had the money, why should I want to spend it to have a good time with the team? My job is to do my job and get home. Not this. I should not be obliged to do this. To have to network and show team spirit as though we are all here to be great friends and upload that happy workplace to Instagram. Why does it matter?

♦♦♦

The exploitative workplace

When you walk into a store to buy goods, you cannot use those goods until you pay for them. You either pay by cash, debit card, cashless mode or credit card. The raison d'etre of the credit card company is to front you an instant loan at a specified interest rate on the spot, should you lack the money to buy those goods. You, as consumer, cannot consume without parting with your money, and there are many instruments and ways developed to make your ease of parting with it convenient.

There is no way in which you may consume goods and pay for them later. Because goods are tangible, we understand this nature of transaction. Because services are not, we do not view it the same way. Employment, labour, is the only transaction in which the consumer—your employer—consumes your services for a whole month without having to pay for them until a month later. Even then, he may evaluate, delay, cut pay, be unfair, etc. as some employers often are with day labourers.

You effectively provide your services for free and gain payment for it at the end of the month. This is why it is called 'compensation'.

So effectively, when an employee is expected to pay from his or her pocket, for client meetings, or travel on the job, lunches etc., with reimbursements to be collected at the end of the month, it constitutes exploitation of labour.

Not only are you working for free, you are aiding the employer who is using your services, from your pocket. Employees who perform these functions for the job need to be compensated in advance. That's not a favour. More employees seemed to know this, where their rights began and the company's ended, in the socialist world. Trade Unions helped set boundaries, for timings, for pay, and for deliverables.

But in an elitist white collar word, devoid of trade organisations that protect worker interests, and in the middle-class aspiration to rise out of the 'worker class' into entrepreneurship, partnerships, management—anything that puts as much distance between them and the ant-like workers of communism and socialist republics—rights of individuals in work places have been steadily eroded. Contracts of employment today are finely worded deeds of legalese that put the onus on fitting in, working hard, achieving deliverables and taking limited days off, solely on the employee.

The employee, shorn of his collective bargaining power, becomes an infinitely exploitable unit. In the employer-employee equation, there is no bargaining power with the employee except the demand and supply of market forces. All aspects of his working life are governed by the length of the queue outside HR's door. When they say that India is a human resource-rich country and make that sound like a virtue, what they mean is, really, that plenty of people want your job, so your rights become dispensable, and your cost as an employee is low. "Please leave, someone else will take your spot." It is, thus, expedient upon the employee to make himself amenable.

In case you thought they told you to dress smart for interviews so you'd look good if they took your picture for the employee ID, the truth is your amenability factor is measured from the moment of the interview on: How you speak, hold yourself, your grooming, presentation, brand of apparel worn, where you live, whether your parents were educated, and whether your educational qualifications conform to those of 'people like us'. The system, thus, picks, propagates and rewards through appraisals, promotions and pay hikes, the employee, who is, thus, transformed into a team player, and becomes 'people like us'.

Yes, that team lunch matters.

"If you don't socialise, you're the 'small town girl from Assam'"

Soma Bhattacharjee, 32, Associate Creative Director of a Start-Up Advertising Agency, Bengaluru

In 2008, I came to Bengaluru looking for a job in the field of advertising. Being from Assam, exposure to such an industry was

impossible. I know what you are thinking — Mumbai should have been my obvious choice. But it's expensive. I was not from any reputed advertising institute neither did I have any experience in creative writing, so it would have been impossible to survive in that city. The mere thought of it scared me. You can say, the fear of being called 'urban poor' already made its way into me. Delhi wasn't safe as my parents put it. And I was taking baby steps towards being independent, so going drastically against them wasn't really what I wanted to do. The only other choice I was left with was Bengaluru.

Soon after I arrived in Bengaluru I realised it was a wrong decision. It was recession time. People were either jobless or struggling. After a couple of months, I somehow landed myself an internship. I was told I'm lucky because at least I was getting a stipend of Rs 8,000. Few months into the internship, I was asked to leave, because they couldn't afford any extra expense. My Paying Guest (PG) accommodation cost was Rs 4,000, and I had to send some money home, being the eldest daughter. I was clueless what to do. I would think of going home, but my self-respect wouldn't approve of it. I skipped meals to reduce the PG rent. My friends used to go to malls and McDonald's' of the world and I would make excuses that I had interviews, while in reality, I had none. My shopping place was the roadside Rs 100-kurtis and leggings, if at all. When I had interviews, I borrowed my friends' clothes to at least look capable of being a copywriter. In this fancy industry, looks matter a lot.

It took me eight months to get a job. It was not a copywriter's job. I was hired as a proofreader in a media house. The salary was Rs 18,000. By that time, I realised I was already in debt of more than Rs 50,000 from my friends and family; borrowed only to survive in the city. On that salary, I had to live and pay my debts.

I got my first break in copywriting in 2010 (two years after my arrival in Bengaluru). And because the industry was coming back to normal, I got a decent salary of Rs 25,000. But that came with baggage of its own. The baggage of working at a fancy advertising agency, where people partied four times a week. And if you don't socialise, you are perceived as a small town girl from Assam ... (you know ... 'ganwar'). You were not briefed on high-value brands while your colleague would be because she spent her Rs 25,000 or maybe less in buying accessories, make-up, and booze; in short, she had a lifestyle to understand such brands.

I had to do something to feel included. I started accompanying my female colleagues to parties once a week. Parties with free booze for ladies. I barely had anything in the parties because that will cost money, even when the bill was split into maybe six. But, still, at the end of every month, I would end up broke. Borrowing money from the few good friends I made in Bengaluru.

It's been six years, and now as an Associate Creative Director in a reputed agency, I still witness history repeating itself around me. I always hear people saying that they don't have enough money. But they have the desire to party, go to fancy restaurants, and wear expensive brands. In order to fulfil that desire, they stretch. And end up never having enough. The only reason being they want to beat the peer pressure and feel included.

As I grew wiser, I realised that the best way to manage your economy is to increase your salary, not the expense. I call it smart living. At least, that's how I survived.

♦♦♦

Bengaluru-based HR professional and compensation specialist Subir Chatterjee explains that when the new generation joins work, they join with multiple pressures. Peer pressure is very high. Real earnings are rarely enough to sustain life in the city and withstand all the social pressures that come with it. This is for multiple reasons, primarily, the surplus talent available in India. "When new talent joins a company, the influx and availability of talent is so high that the company is not able to identify and take measures to retain good talent right off the bat. That will come four to five years down the line, when young people have proven themselves in the system and proven themselves invaluable to the company", he says. Starting out however, the availability of talent pushes down salaries to levels far lower than comparable starting salary rates in the US or Europe. It is a game of numbers.

Secondly, for those who go out into the field, such as IT-based services, app-based and mobile-based selling, for whom customer interaction is very high, the peer pressure is very high, especially if they do have to spend from their pockets and be reimbursed later. Very few and rare are the companies that would supply an employee with advance funds. This also creates an additional pressure on the employee.

Thirdly, Chatterjee says, social pressures of the home and social environment — the need to keep pace with certain social parameters, "from the kind of marriage you are in, to the kind of vehicle you drive, to the kind of mobile phone you own. This has become so integrally tied in with our identities that not only entry-level executives, but senior level executives by their own habits are perpetuating a culture where it matters." To be senior in today's corporate world also means the ability to acquire certain perks with each promotion. This is how the leaders of the wolf pack differentiate themselves from the pack — what is acquired as you rise.

Fourthly, while much depends on the work culture and environment, unfortunately we have created systems, which are centred on perks and rewards. You win rewards for acquiring seniority. To indicate seniority, those rewards are flaunted. Those become incentives for the younger generation of employees. The behaviour that merits that incentive is what is incentivised and promoted and on which all future hiring is structured.

The employee team is a clique and its habitual preferred behaviour is structured and pre-determined.

Setting up office for the office

While some companies pay advances for from-pocket expenses, others reimburse. Yet others expect that employees should bring with them the tools of the trade. Which means, have a working computer or laptop at home, and have a valid WiFi connection, at the very least. Most expect that employees will be available at all times on their cellphones, or are at least checking their emails from home in case of urgent work. This work-from-home culture is unique to India. It is, again, a case of employers usurping the rights of employees and imposing into a space where they essentially have no jurisdiction. Failure to comply cannot result in direct punitive action, but it does result in the employee conveying the impression that he or she is not as "enthusiastic about or committed to their work", as one HR professional put it. This results not only in a less than favourable appraisal at the end of term, for those who draw the boundaries between personal and professional, but it also builds in an additional cost to the employee.

Some workplaces—media, tech, film, traditional industries like finance or architecture, research organisations and start-ups, especially smaller firms—do not issue their entry-level employees with items considered gadgets essential to employment such as laptops or mobile phones. While some offer a mobile phone bill reimbursement, they do not pay for handsets.

The assumption that employers are making, then, is that young people who come in to work at the said company must not only be available to operate to a pre-determined, vague, peer-pressure-oriented class standard, but also function over time, and equip themselves with the tools to do both. Using your services for free and asking you to pay from your pocket, while they defer payment a month later.

It would be funny if it wasn't driving several into penury trying to accomplish their jobs, all the while beating themselves up for being somehow less successful by having disadvantaged parents and/or bank balances.

Not only is the disadvantage perpetrated by education systemic, but the consumerism it spawns to fill the void it creates is also systemic, and the opportunity to earn and stop that gap is also systemically engineered to lean on the employee for all that he's got.

And for some reason, the young fresher employee, too new to the system to want to do anything but fit in, find acceptance and rise in the ranks, is the one blamed for making stupid choices.

The capitalist con preys on the youth as users of education, generators of income and boosters of the economy, all the while pushing them to the brink.

"I dropped my phone, hadn't finished EMIs, and I wasn't getting paid"

Kavita Kumar, 24, Policy Research Intern, New Delhi

I joined a small economics research organisation based in Mumbai a year ago as an intern. I was very excited to get the job as I had not expected to be accepted and I wanted to work with some of the seniors there for the work experience. They told me before joining itself that I would not be paid. I was fine with it. I found a small one-room paying guest accommodation that I would share with two other girls in Worli, quite near the office, so I guess I was lucky. Considering my salary was zero at this point, I was already paying Rs 8,000 for the privilege of work experience. On my first day of work, I was told I would also need a laptop of my own. I was assigned a desktop at work, but as an intern, there were deliverables that I could submit in the evening, or check on, or submit research for after work hours. I could not afford a laptop at that point, so I thought it would be good to get a two-in-one kind of smartphone which I could use to also check my email. I thought this would mean I wouldn't need a laptop and separate WiFi etc. I got it at Rs 15,000 on EMIs when a laptop would have cost me Rs 25,000 at least. Then I realised I had to work on Excel sheets which I couldn't properly on the phone, as I had to plot data. So, my father helped me get a used laptop from my cousin in New Delhi. Now, I had to get a dongle to use from home, another expense I had to bear. By this time, the expenses were already through the roof. I didn't know how I would get through six months, but I said okay, let me stick to it. The office is in a narrow space where I was working on a mezzanine floor. It is a very narrow space. One day while going downstairs I dropped my laptop and it broke. When they asked me to either get it repaired or get a new one, I resigned and returned home the next day. Maybe some of us are just not cut out to work in these kinds of jobs.

♦♦♦

The myth of networking

One of the earliest myths propagated by successors and inheritors of high flying corporate careers is that he who networks shall rise. The lone wolf leads no packs. This is a self-propagating paradigm that seeks to perpetuate the passing down of dogmas. It keeps those who agree within, it casts those who disagree without, and in doing so ensures that specific ways of functioning, methodologies of looking at work, and kinds of agreement reach consensus. Sounds familiar? The in-built caste system of the corporate world is a process of self-selection which furthers the myth of 'people like us'.

All form of corporate expression is oriented towards this: the initiation and weeding out begins at the group discussion for MBA filtering of students and extends to the office clique, the water cooler conglomeration, the smoke break bunch, the lunch gang, the grapevine, pub hangouters, cocktail hour soirées, weekend workaholics, off-site brain storming groups, the let's go golfing groups, annual seminars and conferences and what have you, anything identified as a complete lack of necessity in being there but being there anyway in the name of getting a leg up in the industry.

In its extreme form, it is the entire raison d'etre of the Page 3 phenomenon, in which several have acquired fame and tabloid splashes by virtue of sipping champagne in front of specially-invited cameras, that convince the world the next morning that the people in that space were somehow the most important people in the city. They often aren't. An Azim Premji, who went from storekeeper to single-handedly making philanthropic donations worth 80 per cent of total donations made by 36 Indian philanthropists, has never been spotted clutching a champagne glass and posing for the cameras at a red carpet do. For several who will tell you they came to acquire enough of an in with people to get a leg up in life, there is an equal number of assiduous workers who went home at 6 PM sharp every day and never got asked why they got successful. The entire circuit of life coaches is filled with experts whose entire job it is to teach these recluses, the socially awkward, those who've achieved success without particularly asking for it — from politicians to industrialists — how to be, not themselves any more, but what everyone else says they ought to be and sound and look like.

"You realise that no matter how hard you work, you will never fit in"

Neeti Sharma, 28, Works in a Tech Start-up, from Lucknow working in Mumbai

I moved out of Lucknow after my 12th standard to study English Literature at Delhi University. I then moved to Pune to study journalism. I ended up working in Public Relations. When I got my first job in Mumbai, an internship, we were three girls sharing one room in a shady building in Mahim. It was a six-week internship and we were all of marriageable age. So, every three months, someone would move out and you were either looking for a new roommate or a new place to live. My starting salary was Rs 18,000, but all of it was already being spent in a cyclic repayment of loans. I've seen some colleagues who were always so impeccably turned out but if you looked at where and how they lived — it's just a gadda on a floor of a tiny place in Colaba that they share with five other women, but they'd rather live like that than not live in Colaba. They'd constantly be turning up to work too hungover to actually work.

And should you think that 'it is your work that counts' and all of that, there I was working hard, putting in the hours and I'd be called aside and officially told that my block print kurtas, jhumkas, bindis wouldn't cut it for the workplace. I was categorically told not to dress like that, but to adopt 'more professional clothes'. Which meant Western, polished look, good brands, etc. You had to go out often, be seen as a team player. The office was full of snobs and if you didn't join in, you were left out. That would be Rs 2-2,500 per team lunch to fit in. A couple of us went to a manager and spoke about not being able to afford it, but she only gave us a blank smile and stopped inviting us for anything. That never gives off a good impression, so you will never prosper in an office if you have complained or rejected the prevalent work culture like that. It will always be held against you and you will never quite fit in. Even though I worked from 8.30 AM to 10.30 PM and handled six clients, they will still make you feel like you never fit in. To fit in, I've lived on biscuit packets, skipped lunch, bought shoes and clothes that I couldn't really afford and wasn't comfortable wearing. I left the organisation because I was not treated properly despite all the hard work. Because you realise no matter how much you put in, these are the things that determine how you fit into the organisation.

When I came to New Delhi from Lucknow, I was just a simple dal-chawal-roti-sabzi kind of girl. My father was a government servant. Though he was a humble and restrained man — I have never seen my parents use a credit card — we have never been wealthy, but we have never seen lack. My father came from humble origins. Parents make the mistake of thinking that if I have struggled, my children should never have to. So while they would never buy it for themselves, they do not hesitate in allowing my brother to spend Rs 68,000 on a new iPhone. It's a mental set up that gets inculcated of never having to go without.

So, when you do it on your own, you live in a shabby house with no furniture, you compromise on the things that people cannot see — go without eating — but ensure that the things people can see are visible. In offices where everyone goes for lunch together, you will disappear at lunch time and try to visit the dosa vala so you can eat a cheap lunch. I have learned to compromise, I have lived for ten years on my own, but for my brother, who lives with me and spent four years in a hostel studying for his engineering degree, has never really gone without. So to now live without a television (we only just bought a washing machine, and setting up a house requires investments — a fridge, wardrobes, beds, etc.), he does feel *left out, especially at times when everyone at work is discussing a football match and he's not been able to watch it. He now manages with streaming on his mobile phone.*

♦♦♦

This is not to say people skills don't matter. They largely do. But people skills, the ability to convince a team, whether internally or externally, of your ideas, and get them to back and fund it, has more to do with the solidity of your idea, your amiability on the job, and your solution skill set and vision than to do with any actual buying in to the idea of hierarchy and who is important. If anything, it has more to do with your ability to step outside the box and think with different perspectives.

There is a paradox of bias in the evaluation of introverts versus extroverts. A study, *Recognizing Creative Leadership: Can Creative Idea Expression Negatively Relate to Perceptions of Leadership Potential?*, jointly conducted by the Indian School of Business, Hyderabad, and The Wharton School, University of Pennsylvania, US (published in the *Journal of Experimental Social Psychology*, March 2011), defined it thus:

"Leaders valued 'innovation'; the most and yet, by definition, 'innovative' men, who must think against the grain, are rarely attributed leadership qualities. They are often nonconformist, unorthodox, uncertain, even tentative, like their untested ideas." The study found organisations typically biased towards leadership, and against creativity.

What this means is diligent men, like former Prime Minister Manmohan Singh, whom we once admired for the supposed genius of their ideas, are often 'proven' inadequate for the lack of a pithy quote and a pumping fist.

Francesca Gino is Associate Professor of Business Administration in the negotiation, organisations and markets unit at Harvard Business School, US, and author of the study, *Stop Stealing the Spotlight: The Perils of Extraverted Leadership*. Gino, while researching the effects of quietness on teamwork, found the following: "There is evidence that extroverted leaders are perceived as more effective in the workplace. Our research suggests that there is more to the story."

While that is not to suggest that everyone needs to be an introvert, it is conversely not true that everyone entering the job scenario needs to pressure themselves to transform into an extrovert either. The myth is that either works as a blanket formula. What is more likely to work is your going with what comes closest to your authentic personality and furthering that — something very few have the conviction to do until much later in life. It sounds clichéd but being yourself is seriously the best thing you can do for your personality projection, and your bank balance. Will you lose some opportunities by doing that? Most certainly. But will you regret them? Possibly not. As one interviewee put it, "it is more that networking works for those who fit into and are able to play that visible circuit. It won't work anyway for people who are awkward or bad at it, and if you're coming across as diffident. So why force yourself anyway?"

Then why do or must people network? People network because they need to get their ideas to the right people, to make themselves visible. Networking becomes a means to posit the 'I exist' in an undifferentiated crowd by expanding opportunities to do so. But it is not a level playing field. Those who can play the game with skill, conversation, looks, brand, imaging and positioning get noticed. It's the difference between advertising for the steady hair oil that won't give you dandruff that converts it into a serum that Sonam Kapoor endorses.

"I've now failed at getting a large number of films on Indian screens, and this has been entirely a networking problem"

Samit Basu, 36, Author and Screenwriter, Mumbai

If you think you can go through life just doing what you feel like and meeting people you want to meet, life will very justifiably bite you in the ass. Or you're ridiculously privileged and don't realise the network or access you already have because of birth, or pre-determined connections through school or office or whatever. For me, it's mostly been a process of realising that sitting and sulking about people not giving you things you want is a pointless and self-harming process. So then, you figure out what you really want, which is a good thing in itself, and you figure out what you're willing to do to get it, which is also a good thing to know, and then you do as much as you can afford to, both emotionally and practically, and live with the results. I've found that if I get things I thought I wanted through any non-organic process then they feel kind of hollow when I get them. So then I don't do them again. Sometimes it pays off, sometimes it doesn't. I genuinely believe that you don't have to network to get ahead in life, and I know so many people who network like beasts but get nowhere.

Also, it depends on how people see you as well.

I was once at some awards show where one younger writer came up to me and said, very unselfconsciously, that she wished she had my networking skills because I knew everyone and got name called on stage and whatever. Which was a big eye-opener for me because here was one person who thought I was some fabulous networker, and in my own opinion, I am the worst person in the world at it. But on the other hand, I did know everyone in the room, because I've been in this field for 13 years and have written ten books, and have tried not to fight with people unless necessary. I have never managed to figure out how to use these connections for fun and profit, but to the young writer, I was some kind of icon of connectedness and networking ability – and all the work I'd done meant nothing. But when I write, I am definitely trying to reach outside myself – so are my books just an attempt to network? I don't have the answer to this.

Yes, I've always felt the pressure to network to further my career. But usually it's more the realisation that I should have done a few things, networking-wise, to advance my career ten years ago that I didn't and it's too late now. Which in turn doesn't necessarily mean I would have done them, but just that I wish I'd known that they were things I should have done at the time.

Any aspect of the career where there's community celebration involved in my essential career, which is writing books, such as awards, key festival appearances, contracts, even reviews, could have been drastically improved if I had been a natural networker in my early 20s. But you can't be good at any game if you don't know the rules, and there's also no point sulking about this now in my mid 30s. I think what held me back, mostly, was a tendency to do only things that I enjoyed, and avoid everything that I didn't, which included spending time with people I wasn't naturally drawn to because it would be 'good for career'. I love my work, and I love spending time with people whose company I really enjoy, and I've spent my 20s and 30s doing these things instead of trying to game the social structure of my field. And I find I'm completely happy with this. And I applaud the people who put in the extra effort, built the killer network they needed, and got the rewards they did.

I think the most important realisation that happened on this front along the way is that it's just part of the work, and the way the world is structured now — actually, probably always — it's an absolutely necessary part of the work. And that's all it is — it's not something to either admire or look down on. Unfortunately, this realisation hasn't made me a natural networker — it's a talent in itself — but it's helped me figure out why a number of projects in various fields failed, which is a useful thing to know.

It means that I now know the networking component of any project, and then it's up to me to give it the time it needs or not. Pretty much always it's not, but then I don't feel bad if the project falls apart because not doing what was needed was my choice.

I now feel no pressure to fit in with 'the networking crowd' because I don't think it really exists. It's just a bunch of people trying to get things the way that suits them best. I genuinely admire natural networkers now, the way I admire good dancers. I wish I had their skills.

The need for networking has happened much more in other fields, because you can get a novel written by yourself, but everything else needs people. I've now failed at getting a large number of films on Indian screens, and this has been entirely a networking problem — the film industry is a good example of a field that's completely about who you know. Not completely, obviously, but far more important than core competence at the job. Most of the walk aways have been on the grounds of 'OK, to get this moving, I now have to spend six months hanging out with a set of people and going back and forth convincing them about various things instead of doing any other work' and that's always something I've chosen to walk away from, even though the people were often good people with good intentions. Mostly these decisions were pragmatic ones — I cannot afford to not earn more money for six more months, I have to do something else, or, I might spend six months and still not manage to convince these people that this project is moving in the wrong direction, so I should do something else. I've made some really good friends in the process, and become far more aware of the fact that things not working out for me were really my call at the end of the day. Otherwise I'd have this huge list of regrets and grievances that would plunge me into depression, which is never good for work.

More money is always better, but I've seen super-hustlers who had no money to start with and have insane amounts of money now. It's not about money, it's about time and what you do with it. The money component is absolutely field-specific. Like if you work in a field where people judge you for what car you drive and what clothes you wear, then of course you need money to start with even before you play. Like a high-end poker table. But there are plenty of fields where it's not necessary. Those, of course, tend to be fields where there isn't much money in general.

Is the spectacle of it really worth it in the end? I have no idea, because I don't do spectacle and I don't know the end. It depends on how much you want the 'end' – if you want it badly enough, then anything is worth it. Also, a lot of people really enjoy the spectacle in itself, in a journey-not-destination kind of way. People are just very different from one another.

◆ ◆ ◆

₹7.

Easy Money

I went to my brother to ask for a loan cause I was busted Ray Charles

"Yes, but why did they let me?"

Aakarsh Khurana, 28, New Delhi

I will tell you all the things that I have bought on EMIs for almost no down payment: my iPhone, an Xbox console, my 42 inch flat screen television, I bought furniture from two online shopping portals and some clothes and accessories from Amazon and Myntra. I bought books and they kept delivering them one by one. And here's the thing, because when you take a loan, you're just picking the lowest down payment — my iPhone which costs Rs 56,000 was the lowest at Re 1 — but it's only when the next month comes you suddenly realise you owe like Rs 1.5 lakh on a Rs 35,000 salary. So I've to beg, borrow, steal and somehow make that monthly payment and I've no money to eat or anything. I tried returning some stuff to the online shopping portals but it was too late by then. And now I'm stuck for the next two years paying this, so I've no choice but to go find another job that pays me more, but it really sucks cos I liked my job. But my bigger question is, just because I ask, they'll just keep giving me more?

◆◆◆

The line of easy credit

As of January 2017, spending on credit cards has grown at 32 per cent to reach Rs 49,800 crore, faster than any other segment. Consumer durables are the second highest, growing at 11.8 per cent. Personal loans have grown at 11 per cent. Bank and industrial credit remained weak. Meanwhile, credit to large companies slowed down, with a de-growth of 4.4 per cent.

Writing in the financial newspaper *Mint* in 2009, Monika Halan, personal finance expert and senior journalist wrote: "Money is a choice too. A cappuccino and cake. An hour at the gym. A CRV to upgrade to. A home loan to repay. Money is what money does. Money is power. Money is about choices. The heaviness of a Monday morning. Work begins for some. The ongoing engagement with work deep in the heart of another. The job does not begin or end. Work pays the bills for some. Bills get paid as a by-product of the work for another. The acute burden of money and its importance in this life. The lightness of being and money as a tool to exercise choices."

And choice has never before been as plentiful. Never before in Indian history has it been so easy to avail of credit to achieve one's ends. There are numerous avenues open to young people today: a credit card, a salary advance, borrowings from friends and relatives which has been the traditional first port of call, a bank loan linked to your savings bank account, a gold loan, a home loan, personal loans for reasons ranging from travel to shopping to an interior redesign job, educational loans, two-wheeler or four-wheeler loans, and agricultural loans.

According to the Reserve Bank of India (RBI), personal loans grew 19.4 per cent in value in March 2016 compared with 15 per cent the year prior. CIBIL data says 80 per cent of loans are approved to anyone with a score above 750. Data that differentiates which age group this goes to is not specifically available. But the market is set to boom, anticipating which companies like CashE, founded in April 2016, have begun to offer micro loans to salaried people in the 22-36 age group, supplementing CIBIL scores with an evaluation of their social standing and general financial soundness instead. According to *Bloomberg-Quint*, the target audience for these kinds of loans is 80 lakh people earning more than Rs 2.28 lakh per annum across the country. Typically the young, many in their first or second jobs, caught well in advance of bank accounts reflecting any cheque bounces or shortfalls in cash supply, etc. are prime targets for that phone call direct to the desk landline asking if they need a loan.

"The ease of credit is a manifestation of confidence in the future"

Monika Halan, Consulting Editor, Mint

Our fathers' generation of the 1970s and 1980s could not even think of credit in their 40s, 50s and 60s. If you were smart, you got out of the country. You could not leverage a future income because there was no prospect ahead. The only people who could make money were the people who could game the system, which is why entrepreneurs etc. didn't exist. If you made money, you had to be one of the Ambanis, Tatas or Birlas. People who are now in their 50s are the people who began the process of taking on home loans. We could take them on because we had acquired the confidence in our ability to pay. But even we were very cautious borrowers. We were leveraging an appreciating asset. We could buy it now because of our confidence in our ability to pay. But the collateral itself was the asset. We were still playing it safe.

This generation has seen a very different face of India. So they are moving forward with a lot of confidence. In the larger context, we are also seeing old aspirational countries imploding. The UK and the US are both in distress, whereas at home, there is some distress but there is a lot more hope. So they're leveraging the hope in the future with a lot more abandon. They've been introduced to a new lifestyle and some go overboard.

♦♦♦

The blame is not entirely that of the young to shoulder alone. If banks have such high Non-Performing Assets (NPA), where is their 14-15 per cent profit coming from? It comes from the retail business. "Because there is demand, there is supply. With new technology making it easier, peer to peer lending is a click away", Halan says.

India's recent sharp rise in lending to consumers can, in some part, be blamed on the relaxing of stringent norms that govern who may or may not be given a line of credit. This comes at a time when there is no off-take on corporate lending. In simple language, banks can't make profits off institutions at this point in time, so your income is the scapegoat. You are what they rely on to provide them interest when their other sources are low. So when a telemarketer sells you a loan, a credit card, a great interest rate, he's typically going out of his way to ensure you get what you want, even if he has to overlook a salary-to-loan ratio here and there.

Your spending benefits a whole lot of people. It bankrolls the banks and it boosts the economy. The stock markets go up when consumers spend. That's why a lot of non-banking companies get into the loan business. If the bank which hosts your savings account won't give you a loan, someone will offer you a credit card with a year's fee waived, and if that won't work, some smaller financial institution will oblige, and if they won't, a financial technology company — the fin techs as they are called — are here to issue almost instant online approvals and loans; verification, documentation etc. come later. No, they were not merely being nice to a fresher new to the city. They spot an opportunity.

Swanand Kelkar of Morgan Stanley pointed out in early 2016 that the consumer lending portfolio of the top Non-Banking Financial Companies (NBFCs) is equal to ($92 billion) the retail portfolio of the top private sector banks. NBFCs have a 44 per cent share in automobile loans and a 52 per cent share in loans against property. The strong revival in micro finance shows that small lenders are also on the rise. Micro finance has been slammed in the past for pushing borrowers into debt traps. Default rates for finance are generally low in consumer segments to draw consumers, and in India, it is still low compared to international standards. Personal loans are most sensitive to default. This leads to rise in household debt in specific categories rather than across the economy, as in 2008, just prior to the recession. SBI economist Soumya Kanti Ghosh has shown that the share of personal loans in total loans has been rising over the past two years, though it is still below the 2006 peak.

He commented in a research report published in April 2016: "Personal loans share is currently rising in the total loan portfolio which leads one to wonder if this increase suggests a movement towards a similar glaring situation as had happened prior to 2008 global crisis when share of personal loans increased in total ... loans or does it portend a potentially brighter economic outlook ahead."

What the larger financial picture means for the average 20-something in his first job is that he is both a wilful participant whose spending is boosting the economy as well as its unwitting victim.

₹8.

Evolving City

A working class hero is something to be If you want to be a hero, just follow me John Lennon

Fluid force

Till we comprehend the fluidity of migration, nothing will change. The impact of migration on lower income labour classes is studied, but little is devoted to the understanding of its impact on students or urban white collar migrants, the general understanding being that they are a privileged enough class, privileged to even have an education and a job at hand and a fixed income, so why bother. This is a misnomer because the fundamental nature of migration perpetuates income inequality on all classes. And the understanding of impact on a middle class is to comprehend and have empathy for the human condition. Migrants, by implication, are willing to perform the same work for less in order to have the opportunity to move out of their existing circumstances and spaces. This was as true of the agro-ecological Udupi-driven migrations out of Konkan in the 1960s to the taxi industry drawing drivers from Bihar in the 2000s, to the tech sector drawing youth from Nashik today. Migration flows peaked in the 1990s, according to National Sample Survey estimates. By definition, the migrant is paid less to achieve the same task as his more financially and socially stable counterpart. Ironically, it's often for jobs that locals don't want to take on. Migrants are often competing with locals and with rapid advancements for their wages. As the government advisor to the UK, Alan Milburn, warned back in 2013, white collar workers would be the 'new poor' thanks to displacement by technology. In a market where supply far exceeds corporate demand, all of it impacts pay and what is considered a subsistence level of income.

In 2011, the Manpower Group published a report on the Borderless Workforce. It outlined the kind of migration that was contributing to making India a borderless workplace. Where movement has been limited by regional, linguistic or geographic boundaries, today boundaries are expanding to greater international options, with employers ranging across countries, or domestic ones, with more than just two major metros to move to.

> *"The question is no longer restricted to whether migration should or should not be allowed, but is shifting to the question of how to manage migration effectively to enhance its positive effects on development while mitigating any negative impact."*
>
> — MOIA, Annual Report, 2007-08

Thus, IT professionals from Tamil Nadu are a huge part of the Bangalore tech story, labour from Bihar finds its way to Punjab, and the construction industry in Kerala has a huge North East influx. Domestically, states with the highest incomes and highest economic growth—such as Maharashtra—receive talent, while conversely states with the lowest incomes and economic growth—such as Uttar Pradesh and Bihar—supply the talent organically. Migration in Haryana increased exponentially due to its position as a satellite to New Delhi. Simultaneously, migration increased to Gujarat, Greater Mumbai and Bengaluru. These are among the most rapidly growing urban centres in post-reform India. Currently less than a third of India lives in its cities, it will soon be greater than half. None of this is government controlled, unlike international migration. The competition for limited resources and income opportunities will only increase, not reduce with time. You already have young people not making enough, not finding ease of access to public transport, and having no place to stay. It's only going to get worse.

Much of the motivation behind this urge to explore this freedom to move is not merely enhanced income but a better lifestyle, exposure, the spirit of expansion, both personally and financially. We need better planning, better policies and an overall better comprehension of the lacunae that impact migration. All who wander may not be lost, but the State still needs to provide them with a basic road map, like a trail guide to the wilderness, by which to wander most effectively.

> "...Migrants, particularly those who relocate within India, find it hard to access public facilities. This includes access to healthcare, education, ration shops, clean water and sanitation facilities. This is mainly because migrants lack basic identification and proof of residency, which is important for accessing basic public amenities." – Laveesh Bhandari, India's Talent Migration, 2007, Manpower Inc.

One of the insights of the Borderless Workforce report is that language barriers often compound problems for migrants. Domestic migrants are often shut out of essential services due to a lack of ease in acquiring temporary residence proofs. This shuts them out of essential services, from telecommunications to cooking gas. Know Your Customer regulations keep migrants out of banking, telecommunications systems and utilities. Despite the unprecedented scale of migration we are looking at, we have no real systems to facilitate such transfers of systems, with cities like Mumbai and New Delhi offering some makeshift facilities that are based on the whims of landlords, and are, thus, also unstable services.

Compare these lacunae to accommodation in the West, where basics, from gas to the internet, to furniture, like stoves or utilities, or WiFi, which are essentials for a brisk ease of working, are included in the cost of rentals. As a developing society, our facilities remain suspended between the complete collective socialist format of the pre-liberalised mobile, and the yet to acquire or confer complete independence of the developed model. Fact remains, across the board, the lack of basics that results from moving for employment—from accommodation and food and commuting—remain the migrant's essential and personal problem. So they solve it the best they know how. Compromise and restraint don't seem to occur in that exercise.

None of this will be made clear unless we go back to our definitions of wealth, poverty and success and redefine them to understand that progress is cyclic, a continuum, and does not occur in isolation.

For example: With every progressive year, in the name of beautification, the municipal corporations of cities like Mumbai and New Delhi act against street vendors of food. With the game rigged to the advantage of the real estate lobby, the increasing gentrification of former working class mill districts like Lower Parel and Nariman Point is reducing the options for cheap food. Effective 2014, the Brihanmumbai Municipal Corporation (BMC) banned the cooking and preparation of food items by street hawkers. What this means is that office goers who once subsisted on Mumbai street food, cheap and freshly made on the streets, with dozens of vendors lined side-by-side making rates competitive, has resulted in the food options in such areas often limited to, at its cheapest, a sandwich or a coffee at a Starbucks or a similarly higher income coffee house or bistro. Or at best, an illegally run set up in which there is no focus on hygiene or quality, with neither municipality-regulated cooking conditions nor a supply of fresh water.

Spending on food works out to thousands on a monthly basis. Forcing vendors off the streets impacts their buyers too. Recent surveys show that 1 lakh street hawkers in Mumbai depend on selling for their livelihoods and around 40 per cent of them were selling food. Objections to street vendors have come from the point of view of creating congestion around educational institutions and offices and traffic slowdowns, all of which only look at the benefit and advantage to vendor, and none of which take into account benefit and advantage to consumer. To remove these zones unthinkingly essentially pushes the locality towards gentrification and the consumer into a state of hunger, limiting his access to affordable hygienic food, and keeps him there. By up-scaling the neighbourhood, an entire mass of consumers is forced into up-scaling themselves on the assumption that they have the income to match the locality.

Akriti Bhatia, sociologist who has done her Masters in JNU and PhD from the Delhi School of Economics, Tata Institute of Social Sciences (TISS), and IIT Mumbai, is also working on a programme called *Jan Ki Baat*, which records the stories of ordinary people facing extraordinary circumstances. Hers is one of the few interdisciplinary studies that interlocks economics and sociology with various ground phenomena. Urban poverty can be viewed through various lenses, Bhatia notes; she looks at the informality that applies to urban homelessness, access to space, resources, categories of law and legislation.

One of her studies at TISS, Mumbai revolved around the purchase culture in the suburban rail network. The key to what is sold on the trains is that it is consumed by the working class themselves. A whole section of commuters is able to buy cheap, bargain, and participate in the thriving ecosystem of the train. With new legislation, they are being forced into malls. "What was effectively happening was that the commuter culture was subsidising the lifestyle of the urban poor. Today, everyone is forced to shoulder the burden of the market economy. Most of them cannot afford these malls. That is not merely about having money to spend. You may still find something for Rs 200 in a mall, but there is also the additional poverty of not looking the part. Many people are turned away from mall entrances and those of other such upmarket establishments, for not being dressed the part. The kind of issues that erupt when beggars are taken to restaurants. It is not that they don't have the money to pay for a McBurger. They well might have the cash. It's the poverty of who they are which makes them unwanted and unwelcome. Class is not just about having money to pay the bill. It is also about where one is comfortable spending that money. Liberalism is loud and overt. Include, bring in, they'll say. But this is how implicitly exclusion works." A whole generation that is now expected to smilingly participate in this constantly touted booming market economy as its consumers, is not necessarily welcomed in it as they are.

There are also other rips in the social fabric that occur when such unthinking reconfigurations of areas are imposed. In a survey of the Commonwealth Games evictions outside Delhi University, empirical findings put food vendors more at threat than other kinds. The common excuse is littering, but others include factors of hygiene and caste to oust food over other kinds of vendors. In doing so, important connections between various strata of society are unthinkingly torn asunder. Food vendors are key meeting points for people across caste, class and income barriers.

The assumption is also that an entire technology-savvy generation will, once vending zones are evacuated, just happily enough adapt to ordering food in higher end stores, or online, through delivery apps. There's everything from simulated home-cooked meals to tiffin boxes and Udupi food being delivered to your desk. This is done to cater to the new-found expansion of the young palate. People are getting used to more diverse cuisines. Fair enough. Yet again, many of the apps and services set a minimum spend limit which adds up on a per day basis, whether that's a smoothie or a sandwich or a rice plate. These charges also insidiously pile up on a credit card or deplete a debit card very quickly.

For those just making the class entry barrier, these kind of assumptions made at policy levels, from beautification to ousting hawkers, trigger domino effects that influence everything from living to spending patterns and keeps a whole many people, from vendors to spenders, in a state of hunger.

Prachi Salve, a senior policy analyst with a focus on health, working with India Spend, points out that in developed countries like Hong Kong and Singapore, where cooking is not always an option for the busy executive, governments have worked with street hawkers to regularise and legalise vending options. Licensing includes access to clean water, cooking gas lines, sanitation, and well-lit and green seating areas where customers may eat. What this does, Salve points out, is look at the need for cheap food as an essential to how a working-class city functions, which displays an understanding of demographic and need. The perception of poverty as applying to people, not to circumstances, means that the authorities and policy makers tend to view 'The Poor' in isolation—those that sell the food—not poverty itself as cyclical and continuing in its impact—i.e., also affecting those who consume the food. To, therefore, treat the former in isolation from their social context leads to treating the latter also as removed from the circumstances that impact them. There is no understanding that when you change the variable of one, the hawker, you are also changing the expenditure of the other, the lunch-time consumer, and allowing the spectrum of poverty to continue, breaking down the artificial barrier of income between people. If the government needs to see employment figures rise, it is not enough that people have access to jobs but to the facilities that keep them in their jobs. While this is well understood in the studies of lower income groups, it does not translate to the understanding of the middle income groups, because the studies of poverty assume that once a certain income barrier is breached, all associated problems that keep people in their states of poverty cease to apply.

The migrant white collar workers with no access to cheap sources of meals once the street vendor is evicted from his area typifies best why poverty is a spectrum and not a series of disjointed sets. The fluidity of poverty becomes apparent when that of the one affects that of the other. So, the lack of access to cheap and affordable and nutritious food will remain a problem for those above a certain income barrier as much as below it, because the issue—access—remains across the spectrum.

The stratifying of the city based on income groups implies that benefits may also be accrued to those who qualify to pole vault across these artificially-constructed barriers anyway. In this way, instead of affording basic rights—clean water, electricity, sanitation, food, housing—to the mass of society as a given, they are distributed as benefits to those who can afford them. Society as a whole builds a hierarchy of affordability even for basics. As a result, the young are told that their hunger is self-created and the result of their own stupidity, and therefore, something that they deserve to feel until they reach the point of success. Success thereby becomes inextricably linked with hunger. Have you done enough?

Without rewriting the definitions of poverty, the onus of exiting the hunger plateaus will always be on the person experiencing it and not the circumstances creating it. And thus, nothing one does, no matter how much one earns, will ever be enough. The only way in which this kind of systemic hunger, whether for two days or for two months, in the interest of finding and keeping one's employment, may be understood, is if the issue of hunger as a lack of access spread across the poverty spectrum explains the continuity of circumstances causing them irrespective of income.

A man who has 400 rupees in disposable income for that day may run down, grab a bite and get back to work, whereas a man who has 200 rupees to spend may not do so, creating a hunger deficit that becomes his overriding identity. The lack of access is linked to his workplace, to his sense of well-being, to his being thrust in the middle of colleagues and team workers whom he must keep up with, and the corresponding complete social isolation of everything outside of that framework. In the middle income groups, without access to subsidies and doles, all lack gets translated to direct debt.

Each hunger deficit credit contributes to keeping the individual in that state of hunger till he has come to believe it is not only required of him to work harder to exit this circumstance, but that the crucible of hunger is good for him.

Hunger, homelessness, a lack of sufficient income, the changing goal posts on what 'basics' are—these are social problems and not merely economic or statistical ones.

SECTION III
Brand 'I'

Occupational Shift – Generational Shift –
Paradigm Shift – New Identity

Occupational Shift

Do You Want To Make Tea At The BBC? The Clash

"For me, all employment is just a safety net"

Manan Bhatia, 24, BITS Pilani Graduate, New Delhi

A lot of people go through debt. It becomes a trap. For a year after I had graduated, I had not spent money on anything you would call frivolous: not on booze, not on clothes, not on clubbing with friends, etc. I just racked up lakhs of debt playing poker.

Most colleges have underground poker circuits with a small pool of exclusive members. I was considered a good player in college. Poker is a proper sport; it's not gambling. If you play it the right way, you can make good money. In college, I decided that this is what I'm going to do with my life: I wanted to be a professional poker player. Because we weren't earning, we survived on small stakes — buy in for Rs 100 and get up at Rs 300, and make Rs 100 per hour. We used this money for all our social expenses, mobile phone bills, eating out, etc. The stakes were low, but also one is more cautious when one is a student of the game. I maintained the perfect balance. After I graduated, I started earning money — Rs 60,000 a month. I moved to Bandra in Mumbai where there are proper casinos where you can deposit and withdraw cash. I walked into one of the casinos with a friend. I was still immature. I didn't realise that I was new to the game in the grown-up world of real money. I would stake as much as Rs 5,000. My first three or four visits worked out, I turned it into Rs 45,000. I thought "if I'm already so good, why not move to higher stakes?" I risked a third of my monthly salary. I made a pile of Rs 1 lakh. But poker is a game of randomness. It has many variables. Things are not always in your control, but you think they are. The first time I lost, I told myself I had lost only my profit. The second time, I lost Rs 20,000. By the sixth and seventh time, I had lost my entire salary and maxed out my credit card. Then, I lost my salary for the coming month as well. I told myself "this is just a part of the game, it happens. It doesn't happen all the time." Then, I lost another salary and my annual bonus. I was in a spiral. So, now I had no choice but to recover from it. Isn't this what they tell us when we risk our futures for something we believe in? I played until I recovered a certain portion of it, but the setting had become depressing. Poker is a mental game. When you think negative, you set on a losing spiral. I had no choice but to jump jobs for money now. I moved to Bengaluru to join an MNC. In 2015, I was 23 and I had a girlfriend, but I couldn't focus on her. I owed money on my credit card. I played poker all the time. She even staged an intervention for me. The only option I had was to jump jobs again, so I asked for a signing bonus at the new job — to help me pay off my credit card debt, though I had to sign a bond committing to stay with the company for a year — and I came to Gurgaon. This time, I thought I wouldn't play any more.

But my parents lived in Dehradun, and I was alone. I began playing again. I lost money in November and December 2015. I was making fundamental flaws. I taught myself to correct them and went back in January 2016. I played well. At that point, I was earning as much money out of poker as I was at my job. Again in May, I decided on higher stakes. It worked out fine in the beginning. I earned Rs 1.5 lakh in a couple of days; twice my salary. But then I started losing again. I blew everything. I blew my savings, blew my salary, I went into debt and maxed out my credit cards again.

Here's the thing about poker — it requires you to think positive to win. So, each time I would play, I would look at the upside. Even when I had no money to pay my rent. Even when I couldn't even afford to survive a single day. My parents were at that point deciding on moving to Delhi for my sister, who was starting her studies here.

WHO ME, POOR?

In June and July, I stayed at one friend's place or another. I had no place to stay for about three to four months. I shifted about four times. I was hungry a lot. Fortunately, when my parents finally moved, I got a bedroom and free food.

When I told my parents I wanted to pursue poker full time, it seemed like gambling to them. I even spoke to a psychologist. I wondered myself if I had a problem. But here's the thing – I don't care about the money. I want to represent India at the World Poker Forums.

There is a lot of peer pressure to be successful in our circuits, to be the break out guy. You don't want to just be the guy who did his MBA and got the job in an MNC. To me, this is entrepreneurial spirit. This is self-employment. Poker is an intellectual game. It is heightened mental activity; you set your own working hours and make your money. There were days when I earned Rs 60,000 in a single night. It's a game of risk. If you think about it, so is everything else in this technologically-advanced new-idea era. Every start-up is a gamble. My risks are just more mathematical and absolute.

While I believe I have technical skill, I know I lack emotional control. I know my flaws. I also think I continued while on my losing streak because I liked what I was learning about myself from my suffering. When I was putting down my rent money and my money for food, my emotions got too high and I would lose every hand. I was playing out of desperation. Yet, I loved sitting at the high-value tables and swiping in at Rs 2.5 lakh. I liked the risks I was taking. If I lost everything, I could always go back and be the pinstripe in his boring job. If I gained, I would change my life forever.

For me, everything else, all employment is a safety net.

But sometimes it leaves you in a not-so-right frame of mind. It can be a very dark path. I cannot blame anyone else. Some days, I've played all through the night and called in sick at work the next day. Some days, I've played online from the office during working hours as well.

I now follow the rule to keep a certain portion of the salary for basics and play with the rest of it. It never occurred to me I would end up like this. I am not habituated to being a loser. At my job, I now commute to work for at least five hours daily, in Ubers. In the past eight months, I didn't go out of the house. I didn't go to meet anyone. I locked myself in a cage of my own. I was so dedicated to it.

I now utilise that time to read books.

I will play again. I will risk it all again. I will win again. And when I crack the formula to the winning habit, I will be able to quit my job and do this full time.

♦♦♦

Manan Bhatia, name proudly unchanged, in a post-liberalised India, is the epitome of everything the upwardly-mobile parent of the socialist 1980s wished his child would grow up to have—an engineering degree from a top college, the choice to earn and job hop from multi-national firm to multi-national firm, migration mobility from city to city, and hopefully, overseas, besides personal freedoms. The wealth of choice. The sum, in short, of a boundary-less world of opportunity. A boundary-lessness, which is a deliberate outcome of forces of employment and migration of the age, but that brings with it, a destabilising impact on those who must make the move.

Thus, Bhatia, now there, at the pinnacle of that dream, not only realises he no longer wants that dream, but that dream by itself is insufficient today to make a hero of him. That to gain an edge, he must find an edge to the edge everyone thought he had been lent by his education. When the IIT tag by itself ceased to be the pinnacle of achievement, the IIM tag was appended to it. When both together mean nothing unless you have been picked up by the right consortium of futurism—that potentially ground-breaking company built on an idea promising overnight success—does Bhatia really come as that much of a surprise?

On paper, Larry Page literally woke up from a dream at 23 wondering if he could 'download the whole web' and since then, the world has been chasing the next Google in an impossible idea. The more impossible it would seem, the more wild its success. In a world where the start-up, the possible great idea of the future comes couched in millions of dollars invested in a gamble at best—a delivery service, a room rental app, a cab router, a search engine—that could revolutionise the world and earn its founders millions, is Bhatia quite such an anomaly? Is his ambition of poker any more foolish a risk than the personal loan-funded second hand car evaluation app service built out of a free co-working space in Bengaluru? Don't both invest ridiculous amounts of money, offsetting future profits against current loss, on a risky proposition that no one quite knows will work, with a whetted appetite known as risk? And isn't risk, the great gamble with unexpected returns, the promise of the age?

They are always telling us that we are marching into the 21st century with a plethora of options. We've moved in the last 70 years from an era of socialism and labour unions to the free market and a world economy. From manufacturing and industry to services and outsourcing. Where once the plodding hard chores of the factory worker or the farmer were what defined the linear path to success—the liberal democracy under which all hard work is well rewarded by a protective state—today, they call upon us to have an entrepreneurial spirit of innovation and to be big on risk. From the Big Effort, that you once spent a lifetime putting in, to the Big Idea, that just takes a flash of inspiration and a leap of faith. From the protection of the collective 'we' as a society, the world today pivots on individual changemakers.

The new momentum has opened up a great number of new careers—in fashion and music to new digital media and technology—that weren't viable vocations upto a decade ago. In this new society of fragmented achievement, contributing meaningfully to the collective is no longer seen as what gets you places. The traditionalist, the engineer who hasn't quit his PSU job in 20 years to retire with a Rolex and a lifetime of having paid his insurance premiums leaving his family secure, is no longer the ideal. If anything, he represents a resistance to change and an aversion to risk, which is no virtue. Even if he wanted to, the man who seeks to offer up his reliability, stability, and equanimity as assets to organisations and work cultures is coming up against a wall of rejection.

"I had never seen a cappuccino in my life"

Shamik Chatterjee, 24, remote West Bengal

When I first came to New Delhi, I had never seen a Cafe Coffee Day in my life, and when I went in, I couldn't order anything, because I didn't know what a cappuccino was or what a latte was. I come from a small village in West Bengal and I grew up in a very simple family. I was the first to complete my Masters in engineering in my family, and in 2007, was considered quite the scholar back home. I was the one with the books, the academic bent of mind, great analytic skills, winning debates in school and college. I was, you could say, the pride of my small pond. When I graduated and got a job in New Delhi, everyone was very excited for me. But for me, the whole experience was a brutal culture shock. Here, I was the bumpkin. What was a virtue back home — reading voraciously but quietly, simplicity of mind and habit — made me an object of ridicule in my swank corporate office. I was always awkward and out of place. At first I tried to fit in, but then it started to get to a pressure situation. Even if I was good at my job, the social environment at work was too difficult for me to crack. At first, ashamed of my ill-fitting unbranded clothes, I tried to spend to dress like them, go to the events and dinners they went to but it was outside my social comfort zone. I could not enjoy the things they did, and was an awkward addition to most situations, so I slowly stopped being invited even out of courtesy and soon enough, I was left out. In our education system, they don't tell you that non-career related skills sometimes matter more. That you have to sell yourself to people a certain way. I had the grades, I had great ideas, but who would listen to me if I couldn't do all that? Eventually, I gave up trying. Isolated and penalised despite good work, I was feeling bitter. I kept wondering how I could go back home and disappoint all who took such pride in me. I was spending a lot to keep pace with a life I wasn't even enjoying leading. Eventually, I knew I had no choice. I was on the verge of a nervous breakdown. I eventually returned and found work in a public sector company where I was more of a fit. I am no use to the corporate world.

♦ ♦ ♦

While all who still believe in the traditional systems of what constitutes success do not choose to retreat, and that's not to say retreat is necessarily failure — after all, Chatterjee chose the integrity of his own personality as more important to him than altering it to fit in, itself a strength of character, just one that puts oneself outside the rat race — many continue to live with the severe pressures of the culture shock.

Sociologically, today the middle-class man with a government job he never intends to quit, with his own accommodation and life insurance, is treated like our modern-day loser. He lacks ambition, he lacks experience, and he lacks spirit. The man without a broad range of experience across companies, locations, sectors offers an incomplete worldview. His tweets will be insipid and he will have nothing to Instagram or Facebook about that earns him Likes, or friends, or followers — a common question in job interviews in the media, advertising, and IT industries today. The measure of success has radically altered itself in about two decades for an emerging mass of Indian society.

Wealth explorers

Is it practical to expect that the brilliant successes of a Google or a Facebook or an Apple, poster children of the modern age's idea of wealth creation, will emerge from plodding stability, savings, and nine-to-five jobs? Do we really expect the pathbreaking to be offloaded from traditional boats that may not be rocked by good employees who would never shift their weight around? And is it fair, in the age of enthusiasm for such out of the box creation, to expect future creators to suppress their enthusiasm to join in? On the contrary, as individuals, we are each, now, engaged in a race to differentiate ourselves from that homogeneous mass in which goals came pretty much pre-set—doctor, engineer, lawyer—what were seen traditionally as 'nation-building' careers that marked us each out to be responsible units of family, society and nation. An entire generation is racing against itself to prove that it is *not* that.

The path of paradoxes you must walk is manifold. To break in, you must be the break-out, but to stay in and gain acceptance in the new field, you must fit in. There is no manual that comes with this.

The result is the walking of a new wasteland with no road signs—a departure from traditional industries that come with set ways to navigate them. You have set entrance exams and renowned tuition classes, target companies one seeks to work for, and a ready body of knowledge of specialisations within the field, starting salaries resting at a median, and knowledge of experts who can mentor your way forward. In contrast, the newbie in the new-age career is exploring essentially virgin territory.

"I don't believe in small bricks big walls"

Dhruv Shah, 26, Taxation Executive in a Medical Company, B.Com graduate currently doing his MBA

I live with my parents. A couple of years ago, my father, who was a businessman, had a breakdown. My sister who was as old as I am now took a job and shouldered the family. When I turned 17, I got a job at a BPO. I had enough money to live a good lifestyle even after I gave my share at home. Now I'm a tax consultant and doing my MBA alongside. I still give my share to the family. My daily expenses are coffee and cigarettes. I know what the expenses are, but I go clubbing every weekend and hang out with friends. That's Rs 2,000-3,000 every weekend. If I'm at work post 8 PM on any night, I'm too tired to take the train, so I take an Uber or an Ola, which is around Rs 350 one way at the minimum. After the first half of the month, I am flat broke. Why is going out important? Some of it is peer pressure, around 30 per cent. But it's also that after working such long hours, I want to go somewhere too.

My career isn't for life. I want to start my own consultancy and retire as a partner to one of the big four. I also want to create a start-up. I want to start an outsourcing firm. I want to win big. When my sister got married, she made sure she married a man who would get a steady salary in at the end of the month, even if it was a little less. She stresses on security. I can't live like that. Why settle for less? My official timings keep me at work nine hours a day. At least four days a week I work late. At least once a week I reach home at 11.30 PM-12 AM. I am giving so much of myself to the firm as possible, and someone else is making money off me. I can't risk not giving my family the amount they need per month, so I'm going to come up with the money to give myself a year to make this work. I'll need Rs 2-3 lakh in savings of which I have Rs 1-1.5 lakh from my previous company's provident fund. Why don't I just save what I spend on weekends partying? I don't believe in 'small bricks build a big wall'. That's now how big wins are scored.

◆ ◆ ◆

The new industries, some a few years or a decade or two old, are skill-and personality-based and recruit and reward on those merits rather than on mere degree. They attract talent from various parts of the country in new migration patterns. And yet, the movement within them has not achieved the critical mass of comparability in which you are likely to find others who share your experience of it. Every unit of the new age industries is, thus, unique, and capable of finding immense success or meeting with immense pressures. There is no compass. There is no due North.

Road maps and living wages

If India is in the throes of a Make in India boom and a start-up culture, carrying its young along, then there is the need to, within the boundaries of freedom that liberates its thinkers and doers, back up those initiatives with substantial infrastructure. The kind that will pass down benefits to the founders and employees in material and not in mere notional terms. This means spaces that provide safety, infrastructure like WiFi, desks, sanitation, drinking water, places where cheap food can be sold with its own sustaining infrastructure, efficient public transport to and fro, and street lighting. Sustaining a boom in a sector is not merely hosting international conferences in which various participatory companies have the opportunity to meet. Historically, from the diamond industry in Surat to the textile industry in Mumbai—from *chawl* accommodation to the evolution of Udupi and street food—industry hubs have evolved where the ecosystem has made it affordable and culturally viable for the lowest rung to sustain in that industry.

Tej Pochiraju, founder, Jaaga Sustain, India's oldest co-working community created in 2009 and based in Bengaluru, says it's a problem best resolved by some investment in infrastructure and care of companies. He's an advocate for the living wage.

The living wage is an idea that rose in the Renaissance, as a payment from patrons to employees. It is the idea that quite simply, and it is ironic that this ought to be a thing employers have not yet considered, employees need to be able to make a 'fair and decent' living off what they earn, sufficient to meet their basic needs. It stems from a basic agreement that this wage should be able to cover a nutritious diet, safe drinking water, suitable housing, cover energy costs, transport, health care, child care, education and discretionary income, and emergencies. Some believe it should also set work hours. A number of United Nations, International Labour Organization, and Organization of American States' declarations and conventions have attempted to frame it.

Sounds like common sense, except what you currently have is an income determined by market forces, demand and supply—which explains low incomes in a human resources-rich country like India—rather than any consideration of what it actually costs you to make a living.

Pochiraju, who also runs a farm on which participants work and self-sustain for a year, says he's able to break down the living wage to a unit of what it takes to sustain. The US, for instance, with minimum wage requirements, has a living wage culture.

"If you consume everything you have, you'll never have growth"

Dr Tej Pochiraju, Founder, Jaaga Sustain, India's oldest co-working space, Bengaluru

When there is a culture of debt, the mind is stressed. The cost of living, how to sustain, is basically the biggest stress factor there is. There shouldn't even be a discussion around it. A living wage frees up creativity. To support an industry means to allow its workers to move towards creating, and not focus on 'where is the next meal coming from?' It gets shot down in the political cost.

In corporate culture today, it is the exception, not the norm, that the company bears the expenses of the employee. It is attributed to the simplicity of accounting, that the employee carries the burden of payments on the go, especially in start-ups which typically face cash flow issues.

We've seen the importance of frugality in early days. We are sustainable. We focus on low-cost infrastructure, access to community that brings in skills we need. The kind of networking that actually contributes to growth.

A mistake the young commonly make is mapping goals and trying to reach them by any means possible; it is important to see your means and then set goals accordingly. This should be the appropriate entrepreneurship model. Start small, build on resources. Frugality is inherent to entrepreneurship. Today you have entrepreneurs banking on venture capital funding coming in heavily and then seeing what happens. What we've seen of what works with companies that do succeed is they go slow, start building, save capital and reinvest.

In terms of economics, it is a well-known concept that if you consume everything you have, you'll never have growth. Look at credit cards not as consumption, but as investment instruments.

Invest in something in the hope it grows to something. If you look back to 2010-2012, there was no start-up culture. We only had an inherent consumption culture. The start-up culture boomed because of the crash of 2008.

Up until 2008 to 2009, most graduates from IIM Ahmedabad took on jobs. From 2010 onwards, they began to join start-ups because the old ideas of what constitutes stability had been washed away.

In the UK as well, where I was during those years, that was the time that coincided with a big policy shift with the coalition. There was a shift towards self-employment. The mandate of the right wing, the rise of it that you are seeing globally, was towards entrepreneurship. Unemployment numbers were down, tax breaks were offered for the first two to three years if you were self-employed, there was incentive to initiate a start-up in any part of the country, it was incentivised to boost entrepreneurship, and by companies you worked for till yesterday. You took the tax break, you took the clients off the multi-crore company you worked for as an outsource agent, they had insurance costs and they were shrinking anyway. This created a huge policy shift. This also created the freelance consultant module as a powerful entity. In a beehive module, sustainable clusters generate great power.

But without a living wage or supportive infrastructure, you have an individual running a company with three employees, where the founders don't take money. In the excitement of setting up, people place the importance of making money last. If your salary expenses per employee are Rs 30,000 for one year and you budget Rs 3.5 lakh per person per year, a Rs 2 lakh co-working fee and other expenses, at the very least you need a base capital of Rs 15 lakh. This is at the most basic level. There are next to zero people helping you raise that initial fund. Most of it, today, comes out of and creates further personal debt. Simply because there is no understanding that people have to earn, and sustain, while they create.

Generational Shift

Can You Pick Up All The Pieces Of This Broken Generation? Of Mice & Men

"We are all leading a certain lifestyle so we fit in"

Lisa D'Souza, 24, PR Professional from Kochi and Ahmedabad

We've all been in that position where everybody at work is going out to a bar or to a team lunch, and you know that you either don't have the money or if you do take out the money from what you have, you're going to be struggling for the next few days. Sometimes it's not even the every day things, it's someone's big birthday celebrations that you have to attend and contribute to, or 'now I'm going for a wedding and home for Christmas so a huge chunk of my salary has been depleted which I can't cope without'. Luckily, I've never really had to go without a meal though I have seen many who do. I don't cook at home, because by the time I get home I'm too tired so I never carry a dabba. It gets awkward when everyone else who has brought one asks you why you haven't carried one, or gives you condescending advice on how to make one, and then, after you have answered all their questions, they'll ask why you don't go down and buy yourself something to eat. The answer to that is always 'I don't have the money to eat out every day' which you can't say. So you make some excuse. Also when you do go down, it's that the minimum on everything is above Rs 100-200. Nothing is cheap. There have been a few times when it's gotten too tough and I've gone and gotten myself a vada pav but you can't eat that everyday. I don't order a dabba service because I get bored with the food. We are two kinds of extremes in this world – those who spend, and those who are miserly and save 10,000 out of a Rs 20,000 salary. You see them taking buses everywhere and never eating out or socialising, or watching a movie, and always going home, whatever time of night they reach, and cooking. I like living. I like shopping. I can't eat boring food. I manage to save, but I've seen friends who don't eat sometimes. Till now I've had company accommodation, which runs out next month, so once I start paying rent, it's going to be a huge problem. So we're all in the same boat pretty much.

♦♦♦

Can you be poor if you own a smartphone?
There is no quantifiable measure of how many young people draw the curtains and do not socialise for fear of having to skip a meal. Nor of how many store sneakers in their work cabinets because they lack the money to take a cab or a bus home. In short, how many simmer quietly at seeming to be well off and actually aren't. These are decisions that recede into the background of personal choices. It's not a demographic. It's not even a movement. There are no support groups and no clubs. There is just an individualised coming to terms with. So, why should it matter? Are the incidences isolated or do they affect a wider range of people? And is it relevant in terms of social impact? Why should we not focus on simply absolute poverty, in which the human impact is so much more visible?

Since May 2016, when *The Atlantic* came out with its cover story 'The Secret Shame of Middle Class Americans' by a writer, Neal Gabler, who was unable to afford his lifestyle, several news stories across countries have begun to emerge about either those who cannot cope with living standards, or who put up false façades to camouflage the standards they truly live with.

More than asking why we must note incidences of poverty in plain sight, it is more pertinent to ask what happens when we don't account for it.

WHO ME, POOR?

In a year in which the financial concerns of the hitherto thought of as privileged classes — white, straight, statistically accounted for in employment, welfare and public services terms, in middle America and UK — triggered the emergence of the conservative electorate, voting in Trump with the Republican Party's new-found understanding of the American poor, and voting UK out of the European Union, with Brexit, it would be a living in denial to believe the isolated incidences don't add up to achieve significant momentum.

Many of the tell-tale signs pre-dated the votes. In England, millionaire Lord Sugar triggered the 'are you poor if you own a smartphone' debate in 2015. This was sparked by his speaking out against the absence of 'real poverty'. He said he was fed up of people who claimed poverty but owned microwaves and cellphones when poverty was in fact people who didn't have a shilling for a meter. In the US, it was healthcare. Studies find PhDs in the US on food stamps right next to laid-off factory workers. In Europe, the immigration and border policies' fear of accommodating the larger world for limited jobs affects how an entire Union opens the door. Today, news sites like NBC and CNN have dedicated trackers for poverty in plain sight. That dream home, the car, the pair of sneakers, marriage, the phone, and the hoodie, all once pan-American symbols of doing well and being with it, have long since proved to be not speaking the truth of who owns them and why.

A primary reason for this is that while our indicators of poverty have not changed since poverty was first defined, our indicators of wealth have. So we tick off the television, the laptop, the two wheeler or car, as signs that the person in possession of them is doing well enough. The 'poor' man, so defined by his lack of income to meet basic nutritional and consumption needs, is assumed to be necessarily devoted solely to the universal cause of his upliftment from that state of poverty, even when poverty is absolute. Even where the lack is acute and debilitating, a man is still free to be driven by taste and desire and other tangible human emotions that are no less real because he is beholden to the state of poverty. As Abhijit V Bannerjee and Esther Duflo show in *Poor Economics*, the man in the slum would sometimes prefer to invest in a DTH cable connection than in feeding himself. Recipients of free or subsidised mosquito nets, or water chlorination tablets, or schooling, or contraception, often prove bafflingly disinclined to use them. And economists everywhere were stunned at research that proved that their statistics in fact had preferences and tastes and inclinations. There was little evidence, Bannerjee argues, that in the absence of compulsion, or at the very least pressure, any of us would always do the sensible thing. As John Harris writes in *The Guardian*, some, in the hidden poverty of the British middle classes, would rather go to the salon and do their nails, than pay the gas meter. It's the same instinct that leads someone to look at their last Rs 100 note and head off to buy themselves a beer with it. A man with those wealth indicators may still struggle to make his ends meet, irrespective of class and income. Yet, to read our treatises on poverty, one would easily forget that it's human beings who are faced with these issues, and not just inanimate statistics.

Secondly, what is a necessity in hand for a man on the job, or in a home, is not also always listed as a necessity on government survey forms, and thereby, is not considered one when taking into account definitions of items like poverty. While a cellphone or a television set, a smart jacket or a laptop might have seemed like a luxury in the 1970s — indeed several door-to-door surveys continue to ask if the household owns a refrigerator or a television as an indicator of who is above average income — yet several of these items are today basic to economic survival. The cellphone, and its upgrade, the smartphone, is just one key indicator missing from surveys today. A WiFi or any mobile data connection is another. Possession of these items cannot be considered an indicator of 'wealth' any longer.

India's recent demonetisation of higher currency notes to weed out black money in the economy, leaving the country without smooth access to cash for weeks on end, struck home just how vital digital connections are, across classes and segments. Even prior to moving to a cashless economy, from a vegetable hawker to a beautician to a masseuse and a driver, a phone and internet connectivity have been making the difference between one client per day or several. It is the difference between driving a black and yellow cab to fixed earnings, or driving an Uber with the potential to exponentially surge incomes each day. Within these additional indicators, new social hierarchies are constructed with their own class signifiers. With the driver now needing a smartphone, in the ranges of the middle to upper income classes, a more complex smartphone quickly becomes an easy indicator of conspicuous wealth or fake wealth, one used to set you apart from the class below, and in cahoots with the class above. It becomes that which is used to create the façade of belonging to a specific social class, when in actuality one does not. All you need to do is to somehow acquire the trappings of the new indicators—ranging from phones to laptops to even pub or gymkhana admissions—to upgrade status. In such an environment, the clamour for which phone you own, which address you live at and what spots you are visible in, becomes self-evidently important to keeping poverty in plain sight, hidden.

Thirdly, this is how an entire generation perpetrates the ruse. It is a paradoxical ruse, one in which the perpetrator is both victim and wilful con man. He is trapped by his willingness to play along. That it is perpetrated at all is key to understanding why this form of poverty hides. A later section of the book explains the modus operandi of the con in detail; rentals and easy EMIs being a huge part of it. But what essentially makes it possible is social media.

Being active on social media allows the dissemination of a pretension of wealth even if one does not actually have it.

Posting images of places visited to on Instagram, Check-Ins on FourSquare and a timeline of networking on Twitter and Facebook are able to provide one the illusion of having lived well, the busy life, the connected life even if one does not habitually live that. The multiplier effect of it is exponential. This serves a double function, of being a lifeline to potential earning, the 'dress for the job you want' adage being acted out in principle, and also the much-needed and underestimated mental buoyancy to keep one afloat through the tough times. "If one does not have anyway, one can at least do what one can to keep oneself alive while one waits," as one subject of a case study put it.

The irrationality then of how one spends beyond one's means and why no longer seem quite so individualised a response when viewed in a social context. Economics constantly looks to the view that man's primary response to economic necessity will be rational. But what if Economics needs to expand its boundaries on what's actually rational behaviour these days?

"My love ordered the chicken noodles"

Ankur Singh, 25, Financial Analyst, Pune

Sometimes, a picture with a mug of beer or a 'check-in' at Hard Rock Cafe mattered more than our bank balance. Most of my friends and peers and I were living like that as interns. All of us used to be broke and hungry but seldom would anyone recommend a cheaper or a less trendy place to hang out. The amount of self-built peer pressure was insane. We'd see kids richer than us enjoy a certain lifestyle which we would try to emulate. In fact, during the first of year of my internship, I had saved some money which I had planned to invest in the stock market to get a better idea about it, but I ended up spending all of it on a week-long trip to Thailand for a bachelor party (no, no one was getting married). After most of us reached a point that we would have to borrow money from our friends or ask our parents for money, we realised that it wasn't worth it. That phase lasted for almost two years. I am currently a trader/equity analyst with the financial markets. I have learned a lot about the value of money and am now far more secure financially. I don't frequently indulge in binge shopping or drinking. I hope to be able to pay for my MBA tuition and even accommodation in the near future. But back then the purpose of my social media life was to attract other party goers, not necessarily employers. People judge you a lot based on what you post on social media, particularly political criticism or praise. My boss tends to notice a lot and we don't often agree so now I've learned that the social media image is best kept low profile.

When I was playing to the gallery though, I had Rs 100 in my pocket for three days one weekend. I ate eight packets of Maggi in those three days, one for each meal. My stomach hurt like hell but I could only go to a doctor when my stipend arrived. I don't eat Maggi any more. The worst part was on that Sunday, when this girl I liked was in town and wanted to meet me. So I borrowed Rs 1,000 from a friend to take her out to a decent dinner. That was also my only decent meal in those three days. She ordered chicken noodles. You should have seen my face when she placed her order. I had Rs 10 left on my phone balance, so I didn't call anyone for 10 days. Not even my parents. That was my lowest point. But do I regret spending that money on Thailand? Not really.

◆ ◆ ◆

Irrational who?

The understanding that these indicators need to expand and be more inclusive is slowly gaining ground globally. Lisa Cucco, writing in *The New Statesman*, described it thus: "Even though nearly everything about the way our society functions has changed, we expect that poverty should look exactly as it did in the past. That doesn't stack up; having a single colour television would have been the symbol of wealth in the 1950s — today even middle-income working professionals have cinema systems with surround sound and top-of-the-range TVs, discarding them often as rapidly-changing technology improves. As indicators of wealth change, so do indicators of poverty."

Phones today, are not only conspicuous symbols of wealth, their lack inhibits opportunity and connectivity. And indeed it is so, especially in the informal sector--people who function on the new-found freelance and consultant module. "... Those who do have smartphones are not ignorant, they are savvy, choosing to allocate very limited resources to the ubiquitous multi-tool of our time, keeping essential streams of communication open. The moment a person's phone can't be topped up or a contract must be cancelled is devastating to a person's opportunity," Cucco writes.

The Heritage Foundation, a conservative DC-based think tank brought out a paper called 'Air Conditioning, Cable TV, and a Xbox: What is Poverty in the United States?' Dave Schecheter, CNN's National Senior Editor wrote: "If people own luxury items, are they really poor?" Schecheter has written before to question the formula for poverty that uses a model based on our perceptions of poverty from 1955. "Back in 1995, a panel of the National Research Council concluded that 'the official poverty measure in the United States is flawed and does not adequately inform policy-makers or the public about who is poor and who is not poor'. Alternatives using more up-to-date criteria have been proposed but not adopted for official use, so touchy are the political ramifications of a change in defining who is poor", he notes. In order, the top five items for both the population as a whole and those classified as poor were a refrigerator, television, stove and oven, microwave and air conditioning. From the America of the 1950s to today, those parameters have changed drastically.

In the post-Trump US, economists like Robert Schiller, author of *Irrational Exuberance*, have looked at the Trump victory stemming from an economic powerlessness. Shiller wrote in *The Guardian* in 2016: "Those on the downside of rising economic inequality generally do not want government policies that look like handouts. They typically do not want the government to make the tax system more progressive, to impose punishing taxes on the rich, in order to give the money to them. Redistribution feels demeaning. It feels like being labelled a failure. It feels unstable. It feels like being trapped in a relationship of dependency, one that might collapse at any moment. The desperately poor may accept handouts, because they feel they have to. For those who consider themselves at least middle class, however, anything that smacks of a handout is not desired. Instead, they want their economic power back. They want to be in control of their economic lives." What Schiller says next also echoes the argument raging across the Atlantic on 'can you be poor if you own a smartphone?' "Such voters are also almost certainly anxious about the effect of rapidly rising information technology on jobs and incomes. Economically successful people today tend to be those who are technologically savvy, not those living in rural Wisconsin (or rural anywhere). These working-class voters feel a loss of economic optimism; yet, admiring their own people and upholding their values, they want to stay where they are."

Back home in India, the lens commonly applied to measure extreme and absolute poverties—data on income, nutrition, consumption, spending, standard of living, access to hygienic food, water, public transport, affordable accommodation, healthcare, sanitation, occupational opportunity and competitiveness, and mental well-being, apart from asset class and debt and credit patterns, risk assessment—is rarely applied to a demographic that currently floats between the class hierarchies. That's never where you will find them.

This is especially of concern, considering the youth—and India is set to become the youngest country by 2020 with a median age of 29 years, up 464 million from the 430 million of 2011, with 64 per cent of its young in the working age group—is a powerful statistic in marketing surveys.

They are important in that they borrow, spend, and effectively drive that great boom for the economy that everyone has been talking about.

To make it easier for them to do so, they are extended friendly hands by way of ease of credit, access to future earnings. Optimism and belief in that future is higher than it's ever been. Enthused, the young are taking out loans for smartphones, education, for housing, for apparel and cars, for travel, and exposure—an investment in the self, the building of Brand 'I'. It is systemic, a nudge-nudge wink-wink of positive market forces, work culture, social agenda, as much as of the lacunae in government, opportunity and security.

In India, while the average National Sample Survey Organisation form still comes around asking if you own a two-wheeler or a car and a refrigerator, those no longer have the power to suitably speak to class and income in an EMI instalment and credit driven life. The illusion of wealth is easily built up today as opposed to 20 years ago when credit lines were less instantaneously extended.

When you can buy an iPhone on a Re 1 down payment, it is now possible to accrue debt in the process of erecting a façade of well-to-do-ness. It is perfectly possible to take an Uber to work, but not have money to buy yourself a meal once there.

I once took a black and yellow taxi from Colaba to Lower Parel in Mumbai only to find myself at the mercy of a very sleepy cab driver. He explained he had done a night shift and this was his second day shift. On asking him why he didn't just go back to sleep, he replied, "I was sleeping but my wife kicked me out of the house so I can earn enough to buy a liftoff". It took me a couple of repetitions and a lengthy description of what he would do with a 'liftoff' to understand that he meant a laptop. Where was once the colour television of the 1980s, is now the 'liftoff'. The laptop has lower penetrability than the mobile phone across classes in India. According to a 2015 KPMG study, penetration is just 9 per cent—China is comparatively 50 per cent—and is expected to grow at 9 per cent per annum. Conversely, India's smartphone market is the third largest in the world, expected to hit 314 million users by 2017, of which 50 per cent are mobile only users. There are more smartphone users in India than there are laptop users. The mobile phone replaces the computer for most people. In terms of aspiration today, the class hierarchies all kick in all over again from bottom to the top in those verticals.

Studies show that Apple benefited greatly by being the first to introduce EMIs for their phones, with a rise in smartphone purchases going up 300 per cent. Samsung, to keep pace, introduced the tag line in its advertising 'I bought a Note 2 for zero' when it introduced EMIs. Blackberry and HTC followed suit. Analysts say processing charges are largely hidden. Average processing charges on credit cards go up to 8.75 per cent levied over the principal amount and do not take into account damage or theft. EMIs swallow discounts that retailers are able to offer on upfront prices. The hidden costs outweigh the benefits, but the lure is high for social compulsions, not just economic ones.

The smartphone is what is put on the table or held in one's hand, from café to job interview, and becomes a visible, third limb of individual identity. Keeping up with technology is not merely commercial, it has connotations of a comfort zone in periods of isolation, of well-being, of social belonging, connectivity and of upward mobility.

Consequently, you could dismiss a young person taking avail of that marketing offer to purchase a smart phone as foolish, but to him, where he is standing, it is necessary. The smartphone is the new class indicator and connection to economic betterment, and most would sell their bodies, or go without a meal, to acquire and flaunt one.

What outcomes does this have for society beyond some kid who didn't pay his credit card bill this month and starved for a few days? Well, for one, our wealth and poverty indicators are seismically shifting, and our inability to comprehend the shift wedges between social fault lines, creating political outcomes that seem surprising, and that reveal a very divided society. How could that guy have voted for him, we seem to ask, when the votes have been counted. After all, he seemed on the surface to be doing okay, so what poverty, what struggle and what discontent?

At the bottom line, every vote represents an individual. And to live in denial of that individual's reality because of perceived notions of what privilege is, is a liberal blindness society can ill afford. A comprehension of poverty in plain sight is, thus, as much a political necessity as an economic and a social one.

Paradigm Shift

Them Belly Full (But We Hungry) Bob Marley

When renowned contemporary artist Sudarshan Shetty, curator of the Kochi Muziris Biennale for 2016, was opening his first ever solo exhibition, it was to be the culmination of many months of work at his residency at the Kanoria Centre for the Arts in Ahmedabad. At the opening, there among the most fashionably dressed champagne-flute toting collectors and hors d'oeuvres being served on silver trays, patron Urmila Kanoria noticed a rip in Shetty's simple cotton chequered shirt. In the middle of the rip, Shetty had inserted a safety pin to hold it together. At first, Kanoria was annoyed, thinking he was just being shabby, the typical artist lost in his work who, head in the clouds, hadn't thought to show up neatly dressed for his own opening. Then, his diffidence hit her—Shetty had no money for a new shirt even for his own opening. That night, even as Shetty was the toast of the town, he was 'discovered', a new talent born, Kanoria sent out for some new clothes. Shetty reluctantly accepted them. For Kanoria, it was a lesson, she says, in how crucial it was to support artists who were immensely talented but lacked resources to work in peace and take their visions forward. It became a mission. Today, Shetty, always vocal about his days of struggle, is a world-renowned artist and one of India's highest selling. But he is still a product of his days of lack.

"Put a pin in it, and create"

Sudarshan Shetty, 55, Contemporary Artist, Curator of Kochi Muziris Biennale 2016

...It is perfectly natural to want to dress well, even in a time of lack. So much depends on your own trajectory, on who you want to become and what you want to do. My friend, [artist] Krishnamachari Bose, known for his flamboyant style of dressing, dressed that way even when we were struggling. Not just food, your address, clothing, you work with it to shape you. All of it is not just pressure. I won't sit in judgement on those who invest in these things because as an artist, you realise that your work becomes a sum of your pre-requisite curiosities—your interest in fashion, in social circumstance, in poetry, in ways of seeing. This is true for any field. Your idiosyncrasies come into play. One cannot ask 'why is he investing in an idiosyncrasy?' It is an investment in belief and it is necessary to make that investment in your work. Money is a very subjective thing. Rs 10 when you need it urgently can be more valuable than Rs 100. The market for my work came much later. It allowed me to think bigger but I had already invested my belief in my own work by then, which is what allowed the market to come. At the time that I was not selling any work, I worked in isolation from market forces. I didn't have any expectation. I didn't even believe I would ever make enough sales to even own an apartment. But we became a community in our struggle, doing without, and we had a great time. We created for each other and ourselves. You invest in that stage to trace your trajectory. You know its usefulness and functionality to who you need to become. Anyone can go through a monetary struggle, the real struggle is to invest value in what you are making. I was full of doubts, but it is never about the money. Money is incidental to the act of striving for happiness.

I am not saying money is not important. It allows you to scale up your work—I think differently if I am spending Rs 1,000 to create a work and Rs 10 to create a work, so it absolutely does impact how you work—but young people today are too keen on a specific kind of success. Success can be measured in various ways. For some, it means making X amount of money. For others, it means having shown at the Guggenheim. There are varying perceptions of what success is. It is making money that is measured. If we can, remember that money is a tool that no one quite fully understands: someone is always richer than you, and you are always poorer than someone else. Money for some can be an end in itself and that does not necessarily stifle creativity – some like to create in order to sell. Money becomes a part of the work. So, how do you decide what success, and correspondingly, failure is measured by?

I look at what makes you happy. I have been happiest when I have found a new way of doing something. It gets followed by practical problems – where can I show it; since participation of people with my work is important, the number of people who come to my show; seeing it in the possession of a collector – there are various ways in which to extend that state of happiness that rival the origin of the idea itself. Everything is incidental to this. Even money.

◆◆◆

The Wolf of Wall Street Paradigm & the Starving Artist Paradigm

There are two aspects to success: looking the part and living the part. The former is the Wolf of Wall Street Paradigm, the latter is the Starving Artist Paradigm.

In *The Wolf of Wall Street*, the book, Jordan Belfort writes: "Act as if! Act as if you're a wealthy man, rich already, and then you'll surely become rich. Act as if you have unmatched confidence and then people will surely have confidence in you. Act as if you have unmatched experience and then people will follow your advice. And act as if you are already a tremendous success, and as sure as I stand here today — you will become successful."

Like a coach to a team, this is how we mentally psyche ourselves — the power of positivity and all of that life coach-worthy stuff — to meet our goals. We are constantly told to dress for the jobs we want, except no one tells us we must do this on the salaries we have. The gap between the two is what gets typified as the 'struggle days'—a highly romanticised period of doing without.

This is what results in the Starving Artist paradigm. You can only bridge that gap and bite the very painful bullets you have to rationalise the hunger and the homelessness because you've romanticised the living of the pain.

In the Hindi film *Dear Zindagi*, directed by Gauri Shinde, the pop psychologist character played by actor Shah Rukh Khan counsels the lost millennial played by actor Alia Bhatt: "Your generation pushes itself to pick the most complicated path. It's almost as if you feel like you have to punish yourself. Don't make things complex, don't keep searching for the most difficult way. It's okay to take the simplest route to something." Don't let the past blackmail your future, he also adds. It rings true to a generation that is moving from a socialist hangover state and society into a liberated empowered consumerist one. Some of it is also punishing oneself for inheriting the path to a bright future.

There is an essential element of needlessness to this looking and living that differentiates it from genuine struggle. The kind that solid gold breakthrough stories are made of, which everyone aspires to, but few truly have.

Everybody loves the story of genuine talent rising against all odds. These are the tales of self-belief that do not reveal their trajectory till an almost Grecian moment of epiphany. These are the glorious stories of human triumph, neglected talent, and sheer life-changing luck that have become a leitmotif in sport, in industry, in medical and scientific discovery, and which we have come to recognise in the meteoric rises of our most iconic stars. This is the stuff of magazine front covers and Oscar-winning cinematic biopics.

By this, in popular culture and imagination, and most possibly, rightly, we have come to define what success and the path to it definitively looks like.

What it looks like is the 'Chaiwallah' Prime Minister. It is the Dhirubhai Ambani chawl-to-Antilla climb in two generations. It is the grocery store to India's largest philanthropist, Azim Premji. It is the Chennai to PepsiCo, Indira Nooyi, and the Rs 80 to Rs 6.5 billion turnover, Lijjat Papad that brought wealth to a group of uneducated women. It is the Aligarh to Paytm story of start-up poster boy, Vijay Shekhar. It is the Chan-Zuckerberg investment in Byju's app-based e-classes.

The garage in the psyche of the start-up is so romanticised as a symbol of rough origins and tough times, of making do and pulling it together, that it now plays the role of the visual motif in every success story written. It seeps into the architecture and design of many a start-up's grunge look, from peeling wall paint, deliberately chipped cement, to warehouse-like settings and distressed furniture. Why does every hipster hangout joint typify the struggle? Because there is value in stripping the finished product of its sheen; a glossing over has come to diminish the value of the success. Worn proudly like a battle scar, without the distress, without the hand-held camera shots, and the deliberately non-stylised use of resources, office space, equipment, how will the counter to the mainstream rise, how is anyone to recognise that it is a success at all?

That artists must struggle to create is one of the oldest tropes of both a bohemian freedom and a democratised success. In the age that combines both in our environments of accepted lack, it is almost expected.

Struggle was first made fashionable by Henri Murger in his 1851 novel *Scenes de la Vie de la Boheme*, a series of stories, almost case studies of literary circles in which young people lived lives of excess and a lack of frugality and order, which becomes integral to the lives they lead and the works they need to create. The theme was furthered by Puccini's *La Boheme*, in Franz Kafka's *A Hunger Artist*, and Virginia Nicholson's *Among the Bohemians: Experiments in Living*. Through popular depiction, the eternal glamour of former billboard painter M. F. Hussain walking around barefoot even as his art sold in millions all over the world, the artist and the creator of immortal success has been painted in arching irony, as a man all-too-willing to compromise on his needs. He does not eat, he does not consume, he does not want, or should not, and only through that crucible is his act of creation made supreme. The romanticism of this Starving Artist Paradigm percolates down to how that money is spent when it begins to be earned. Your first earnings are invested back into your work—into much-needed paints, into dream canvases, a small studio, into renting a villa by the seaside, or on a mountain top so that one may have the right atmosphere in which one may complete one's work, or into the fashions of the circuit and the glamour of the explorations in the belief that, like the showman artist, a little bit of marketing and networking can only benefit sales. It is not just success that a modern generation is after, it is a particular kind of success. To have failed to tap into the multiple opportunities and intersectionality that life offers up today, is to have not lived at all.

Yet, this is not entirely wrong. Art subsists on the gallery system, on sales, and on visibility, much like any other line of business from film to literature as much as theatre or fashion—and make no mistake, ultimately, art that does not sell is at best a home project. Acceptance into the mainstream becomes as critical as breaking away from it. It is a myth that democratisation of opportunity suddenly throws up all manner of stars. The traditional systems that weed out the less equipped are often valid systems. As Germaine Greer put it when addressing a literature festival in Mumbai in 2015, "I keep looking at paintings on the pavement outside Hyde Park and am yet to discover evidence of the next Rembrandt there". Yet, the paradox is that even as your success is eventually defined by your saleability, the money you make off of your talent, the entire ecosystem that thrives off those very sales continues to perpetuate the myth of art for art's sake. The modern day artist, whatever his field of work, must display this willingness to struggle in order to succeed, the ability to sacrifice material wants, even as you seek material gain.

We are at once a society selling the top line — the idealism — as much as the bottom line — material worth.

Within this paradox, the Starving Artist fits with ease into the Indian cultural context. Here, where generations are just stepping out of systemic poverty, finding their way around new towns, and in new-age vocations, from fashion to music, start-ups to software, many young migrants arrive without guidance from those who may have gone into those streams before, and find themselves needing to invest in the career to establish themselves on level with other players at a home-ground advantage — those who live in the city, have family or friends to guide them, and are entering a known ecosystem with confidence. Buoyed by the successes of the rags-to-riches tropes, the average Indian dreams of exiting his ghetto, passing successfully through that crucible of suffering, and achieving the pinnacle of wealth. It is an integrated dream. Consequently, the investment in suffering is as conscious and deep as the returns on investment in rising out of it.

This struggle is typified and glamourised in Indian cinema. From Akshay Kumar who went from street-side stall cook to film star who saves India in every film to Shah Rukh Khan who followed his lady love to the City of Dreams and won, not the only the girl, but built his mansion facing the sea and became a superstar. It is reflected in the plot lines of films such as Guru Dutt's *Pyaasa* (1957) in which a struggling poet gains fame after death. It is evident in Hrishikesh Mukherjee's *Satyakam* (1969) in which the middle class hero jumps jobs to avoid dishonest compromise. You will find it in Ashutosh Gowariker's *Swades* (2004), in which the NASA-returned scientist altruistically electrifies a village, and Mani Ratnam's *Guru* (2007) based on India's most iconic entrepreneur Dhirubhai Ambani. It is evident even in yuppie seeking-the-self films such as Ayan Mukerji's *Wake Up Sid* (2009). The idea that all deserving success must be preceded by a period of struggle is entrenched and glamourised in our collective psyche. The doing without, even if one has access to resources that one may tap into, is perceived as a necessary process for growth.

Struggle per se is not bad, nor is every struggle inauthentic. The problem arises when we create systems that not only expect visible signs of the struggle but deny the successes of those who posit a different kind of struggle, one outside the cinematic paradigm.

A formulaic virality

By making rags-to-riches success stories modular, they are retold in multiple mediums over generations and chisel into public opinion what success is, how it is achieved, and who the successful are. We do so to make success a capsule, like everything else in a consumerist society, in order to ensure that it is easily replicable. Even the break-out guy must become formulaic in order to create a multiplier effect. In its potential ability to go viral, is its aspiration value. The pressure is now on to be that break out guy, who is no longer the outlier, but in danger of becoming the formula.

However, by doing this, the impact of its flip side often escapes us: all other kinds of success, and other possible paths to it seem de-glamourised and fall into the zone of 'not quite so successful'. Is the non-modular success, a quiet success, a less dramatic success, and a less telling success, success at all? And can we recognise it when confronted with it?

Sujayath Ali, CEO and co-founder of Voonik, one of India's first online shopping portals that helps demystify fashion by connecting stylists to customers, already one of the steady success stories of the start-up world, has always remained shy of the limelight, though he is well known as a model of what success should ideally look like. He began to set up Voonik at the age of 32; he posits a more conservative model of what success means. Voonik came on to the scene before Myntra did, and set the way for shopping portals in

India. There was no drama to its success. It was a solid idea built by two former classmates on a sure and steady footing. And that doesn't mean that Ali didn't struggle, have to make his way up, or had it easy. He did them all, made mistakes, learned from them, recovered and made it big. The difference is Ali didn't pitch his and his company's image on making the struggle his USP.

Founded in 2013, Voonik acquired $20mn in its second round of funding. It has recently become big enough to acquire portals like Dekkoh, Zohraa, Picksilk, Styl, TrialKart and Getsy. It's about as solid as start-up success gets without yet being the everyday name-dropped poster boy story. It's rarely on page one for its quiet creeping acquisitions, but it also will never be on page one as a potential disaster in the making.

"In reality, as with Bollywood, only 0.1 per cent make it"

Sujayath Ali, 34, Founder, Voonik

People who know, know what success takes and that it doesn't come overnight. Perhaps the perception is that start-ups gain overnight success and big money. There are two kinds of people: those who set up their own companies, and those who join start-ups. Where start-ups speed up the process is where it would take you 15-20 years to head a company in the mainstream corporate market, you can achieve that right in four to five years here. But monetarily, to set up your own company is not as lucrative as joining a corporate job. So how you view and manage money matters. The year 2015 saw many cases in which the founders were not able to pull their money out of the set up and lost heavily. You have to understand that when a founder gives up on his company, it'll only be after trying everything possible, which means he would have maxed out all his credit cards, accumulated debt etc., which is why most of these guys join a corporate job when they shut shop — because they have to pay their bills.

Interestingly, joining a start-up is not that much of hard work. Sometimes companies that have received funding get into hiring mode and take on ten to 50, even 100 recruits. The company has suddenly scaled up and where there were 15 engineers to work with, there are now two or three times that. Not everyone knows how to do that scaling up. Any company takes time to adjust. So for six months or more, there will be misallocated resources, people who are paid a lot and don't have enough work to do, etc. It's only after the company settles into the new mode that a company realises it may have over-hired. There's also the issue that freshers need direction, but start-ups tend to look for self-starters, people who can take the initiative and don't wait for direction. In the mismatches, lay-offs ensue. Since start-ups are not able to offer stability, they compensate by offering higher compensations to new joinees.

Where people start to throw their money around is when they have stock options, ESOPs and imagine that when the company acquires equity, goes for an IPO, they are going to be rich, so why save? Most people starting out with ESOPs think they don't need to bother, so blow all their salaries. Many who come straight out of IITs etc. start with a Rs 20 lakh salary. A lot of people have not seen that kind of cash at the entry level and it is not uncommon that they find themselves severely in debt in one to two years.

What is really needed is to have the ability to learn. Start-ups are a huge learning curve, so to ride it you have to be able to read the situation and adapt to it, which most founders are not able to do.

The mindset in the last four to five years has been to over-glamourise start-ups, which was good for us, because it turned it into a hub-based industry that was able to attract a lot of talent. But that also made us a hub, like Bollywood is a hub for films, and what happens with that is that a whole lot of people get drawn to the glamour and all the hard work goes underground. In reality, as with Bollywood, only 0.1 per cent of those who struggle have a hit on their hands.

The media essentially functions with a time lag, so now, with some of the start-ups that have faltered in 2015, the horror stories are coming out, but it'll take time for that to correct the picture that was created.

◆◆◆

Democratisation of talent

While not everyone may have their company name turned into a verb, point is they don't need to in order to be successful. Modern hyped up definitions of success seem to miss this, making the end of all success being what goes viral.

Having said that, the benefits accrued from the democratisation of social impact that results from social media—Twitter, Instagram, Snapchat and Facebook—signify that anyone has the *potential* to achieve such virality, and as such, be noticed. Virality by itself, thus, is not misplaced, or achieving that kind of success, so long as we are clear it is just one, equally valid, form of it as other kinds. It has worked wonderfully for many.

Sofia Ashraf, the rapper from Chennai who launched into song about Kodaikanal's fight against Unilever's environmental pollution, became an overnight social media name. All India Bakchod, the comedy collective eschewed traditional media and found their cult following and fame and money, entirely online. Gul Panag, former model and actress, turned her political career on her newfound online image.

In limiting the definitions by imbuing them with traditional reward status, we forget the young upstart with a great idea no longer needs a magazine cover to be declared a success. That is the whole point of disruptor models. In making the magazine cover a reward for the lack of need of it, we defeat the purpose of expanding those definitions.

The talent construct

On the flip side, the benefit is the system now accepts only those success stories that come in the form of these modules, in order to be noticed and counted. This is both a merit and a demerit. While this has opened out the playing field for *who* is eligible to be noticed, this effectively opens out the platform to the thousands and millions with an undeniable variety and range of talents. Job offers can come to you via Direct Messaging through a potential boss or HR trawling different forums/channels for new talent and reaching out to those even without traditional qualifications for a specified job and without the candidate having gone through normal application procedures. What this also means, is what now goes viral and gets noticed nationally and internationally, is a competition for eyeballs with a cat video. Being noticed does not necessarily imply that you are the kind of success you are hoping to be, and your competition is much wider than you would have faced, if you were to be picked discerningly out of a room of 100 talented people come to compete for a single paying position.

Bengaluru-based Social Media Consultant Gautam Ghosh explains that some of this is exaggerated perception. Social media is of prime importance today in industries where it is integral to the work, with visibility and reach, such as media or filmmaking or even politics and image communication roles. People who work freelance and in visual media like design, can use Instagram to find new clients that were previously beyond their reach. Even in software, to some extent, great coding on online forums opens one's talents up to off the cuff hiring. But for a mass of the workforce, social media, mostly LinkedIn, doesn't really impact jobs, hireability or pay scales, and traditional hiring methods are still followed. "There are probably two people on social media who will make it to the level of CEO because of a strategic use of social media, so it's not a mass tool. But where it does work is that when someone strategic, thinking and talented is able to wield it well, the magnifier effect is amplified as to create a break-out success", he says. In short, the riskier risk on social media may not always work, but when it is taken with the right strategy, it can win you big. Ghosh points to people in non-traditional careers, like chefs, such as Manu Chandra of Monkey Bar and Olive or Chef Thomas Zacharias of the Bombay Canteen, who are able to amplify their presence and their brand identities through the use of social media which makes them larger than life in what is otherwise a back room, closed door occupation visible only to maybe regular clientèle.

So, he who would be noticed today then needs to be as much strategic as he is talented.

"Success today is a construct," says Tanuj Garg, a veteran industry expert and film producer. "The days of the great Indian superstar are over. There will never again be that kind of glamour because it is not possible to carve that kind of iconism out of the current fan base. In an essential information age, actors can no longer remain aloof and build a mystique and aura that limited media once made possible. Social media is like the reality television camera—it makes everything all too real, revealing and intimate. The business of acting today is also cocooned by publicists, managers, and image building by both production companies and the star's own staff. There is no 'being real' that is spontaneous. Twitter and Instagram feeds are run by teams. Facebook page followings are carefully monitored and enumerated as part of a star's annual net worth. Therefore, all image and stardom today is a careful construct." Garg also explains that there is a flip side to all that image construction that the cadre of stars and their entourages manage to manufacture so well. "Social media has also given birth to a host of non-entities who have become famous in real life merely for being on social media and using it to its advantage. Amusingly, we've even devised a tag for them—'social media sensations'," he says. If stars can morph into superstars, stardom today, with the right tools, the look, imaging, social media channels and clever manoeuvring can make stars on non-traditional platforms out of the rejects of other traditional ones. And who doesn't want that?

How the paradigm perpetuates the struggle

Instead of finding better improved ways to support young workers and nurture their ambitions, the pressure on young people is starting to wring them dry.

Much of this stems from our lack of understanding of the young, of how cities work, the need for public spaces and support systems, or indeed, of migration and employment itself. We don't quite fully understand the ways in which technology amplifies visibility and yet impacts communications. People are as lonely as they are connected. Are we more social or less now? Who knows for sure? But it's on an entire younger generation to find out and bear the brunt of it.

New Identity

> **Y'all don't know my struggle**
> **Y'all can't match my hustle** Kanye West

"You're spending outside your comfort zone, if not income zone"

Raja Ganapathy, 45, Director-Marketing & Communications, Sequoia Capital

One of the unique features of cities like Mumbai is the proximity of the very wealthy and the very poor. You have Mercedes and Audis coming out of high rises into chawls and slums that face them. This cheek-by-jowlness of modern life propagates an inequality that creates grievances. It becomes very hard not to ask 'why am I deprived of this life?' Inequality is the equivalence between one month's salary and the cost of one dinner, and yet, to have them interlinked such that each – the very wealthy and the very poor – depend on each other for their survival, is the paradox of modern life.

What we are witnessing today has little to do with the much maligned start-up culture and more to do with how life has evolved in these gaps. And much of the consumption behaviour you refer to stems from the 'hangover of wants' that we carry from childhood and this, I believe, accounts for a lot of our drive. I see this as an integral part of the process of evolution.

I grew up in a middle class family with severely conservative values, as most of us did, where we did not eat chocolates whenever we felt like it, and jeans were not daily wear and indulgences were an annual affair at most. So while our needs were fulfilled, there were many wants kept pending. We do not come from a culture where our every want merits fulfilment, and so we carry a hangover of wants that we'd like to see finally fulfilled. Most of us continue to carry that value system forward, in that I continue to look at the right side of a menu when I go out, even if I am better off today than I was then.

When I joined my first job, in advertising, a field known for its flamboyance, I felt a lot of social pressure. I was an anachronism. I could not dress well and I was one of three people in the management cadre to take the bus home, because I could not afford anything else and because my value systems would not allow me to. It is inevitable that you will eventually bow to that pressure. I would leave late at night so no one would see me take the bus. People would suggest casually that I take a loan and buy a car. I eventually graduated to taking an auto rickshaw. I began to upgrade my clothes. Our environments pressurise us to belong as most human beings want to conform. If advertising was showmanship, the corporate world of banking has a more formal compulsion to fit in. When I moved to a multi-national bank after ten years in advertising, I remember a colleague whose spectacle frames were slightly cracked being asked why he hadn't fixed them yet. "Do we not pay you enough?", the boss asked him, in front of everyone, as we looked at ourselves and each other, aghast, more afraid at being brutally called out next. It is inevitable in such environments to be driven to consumption, which if it is not outside your income levels, is outside your comfort levels.

To me, this is why start-ups are so different and the 'start-up culture' so much better. At heart, all founders are hackers, not just from a product perspective but from a life perspective ... Because the Start-up, in this context of received culture, is the one place where it is cool to not be dressed up a certain way. The Start-up guy is, by nature, the guy who has hacked himself a great deal or found himself discounts online. You'll never hear him boast of paying full price for an Armani suit, more likely he will laugh about hacking himself a month-long discount at Dominos. If I look around at some of the founders I have worked with – from Sujayath Ali (Voonik) to Kunal Shah (FreeCharge) to Byju Raveendran (Byju's) – they dress the same, work the same, speak the same as before they hit success. They are essentially 'life hackers'. I learned that word from a start-up founder and I love what it represents. To my mind, everything else is the exception, not the rule. The start-up ethos is about not paying attention to what went before, and the generation that went before that defined how things had to be done.

Indulgences per se are not wrong. They may be wrong for me, but they won't be for my child. It's a very different generation out there today, far far more optimistic. If you had told me ten years ago that I would live in a certain kind of house and drive a certain kind of car, I would have said 'no way'. Today's generation can conceive of possibilities ten years down the line far more easily, and that reflects in consumer behaviour and spending patterns. They also do not believe in getting there 'one day'. If one can get there 'one day', one should be able to get there now. They are short on patience and high on drive. Given this, I strongly feel that all debt is not necessarily bad. It means we are leveraging the future in an optimistic environment. The only thing we lack is patience, to know when to take on debt and how much and for what reasons. But truth be told, I like reading these stories of debt and struggle. They are not negative, but positive.

If anything, I believe the start-up culture is the thing keeping everyone sane. It is giving rise to an entrepreneurial spirit that speaks to the success of plodding hard work and long term creation of wealth and value. I was watching an interview of Uber founder Travis Kalanick, where he said how today Uber is a $60bn company and he hasn't moved out of the house he lived in when he founded it, nor has he sold a single share of Uber in the last ten years. That is the passion, intensity and integrity that founders who create successful start-ups bring to the table.

So, there is clearly a stark difference between what is 'perceived' start-up culture and what it is. Are there those that have mistaken the perception for the reality? Yes, there are start-ups that have made mistakes. That is a tragedy, but we need to cut them some slack. For a number of reasons:

First, the media hunts for a certain kind of success story to populate its magazine covers. And those that do not fit that mould get called 'failures' or not quite as successful. But here is the thing, the start-up culture has allowed India to learn how to fail. We came from a culture where success at all costs is so ingrained — get that degree, join that company, get that salary, buy that house, that car, lead a certain kind of life — that the start-up's ability to fail and rebuild on that failure is an invaluable lesson for us socially. I joined a start-up in 2000 that crashed in the first dot com bust. I was initially embarrassed at the failure and used to bury this stint in my profile. Not any more.

Secondly, it allows us to re-frame what constitutes success. To comprehend that there is not just one kind of success. The media narrative, the cinematic narrative, all seek the rags-to-riches story, the dramatic arch. It locks success and failure into binaries. Whereas, if you look at the real success stories of the start-up space, they do not all have the drama that qualifies their story to be told. Nor do all of them pay attention to marketing their stories.

Third, it all speaks to a loss of patience in this age. Overall, we have lost patience. Things must happen now, the arch needs to be narrated in a specific time frame and module. It is worrying that we are not willing to wait. If we are buying things we don't need and are overreaching, it is because we are not pacing ourselves. So it's not just media, but also the quest for dramatic evolution, spurred in turn, by the lack of patience of the consumer.

As VCs, life for us is long term. Patience has to be inbuilt into the backbone because you enter a company very soon and exit very late. There is rarely immediate success. Success is rarely about who raises what kind of money. Money is not the differentiator. Money has never created anything on its own. It's about intelligent use of lean capital that comes with great company-building skills. The extension of technology to this end is merely a tool. And don't blame technology for spurring conspicuous consumption. Copious spending is never the fault of the instrument, which at best amplifies the speed by which human nature achieves what it had always intended to.

If anything, start-ups have helped redefine success in India. Parents are waking up to the idea that being an engineer or a doctor and having a certain bank balance aren't the only parameters. So, I wish for our children that they have everything they need but not everything they want. Knowing what exists and what is out of reach creates drive and pursuit. And that by doing so, they arrive at their own definitions of what constitutes success for them.

I met P.V. Sindhu at Gopichand's Academy in Hyderabad and she was telling me she has no friends, doesn't watch TV, has no life to speak of, and shows up for training at 4.30 AM every morning. Her parents don't force her, but they enable her. And she is so brilliantly happy doing what she does. That way of defining what success is for oneself undoubtedly calls for sacrifice, whether that investment in ourselves takes the form of money or other equally difficult deprivations. We are slowly attuning ourselves to the fact that you can create that definition for yourself, take an idea and run with it, can fail at it, can pursue dreams and still achieve success.

◆◆◆

Building Brand 'I'

In this paradoxical environment, where the disruptors are those building up, the happenstance of success has to be grabbed by any means possible. And for that to happen, you need an eyeball-grabbing story. The average 20 something year old, who seeks to be noticed is, therefore, engaged in a similar construction of himself into a quasi superstar. He is weaving for himself a story, a look, a projection, a narrative composed of visual and verbal queues – images that speak to his aesthetics, one-liners that speak to his wit and erudition, travel, exposure, the company he keeps, how happening his life is, etc. In this initially conscious and subsequently self-automated flow of imagery, the story of who we are is tilting at the windmills of success.

The most available to the mind module is the rags to riches, success against all odds, the survivor, these are time-tested, assured of being told and retold with some visibility in the end, when the success has finally come. In an era crowded with voices seeking their tales to be told, it is a formulaic ladder.

Culturally, we also comprehend struggle well. In common folklore, in legendary family banter, the stories best told are of parents or grandparents who came to town with 'Rs 20 in his pocket and a dream'. This not only makes us susceptible to the myth of 'this is how it is done', but also entrenches the belief that no dreams are out of reach, and all struggle is valid. The Indian ethos of migration out of spaces of lack, whether of resources or opportunity, makes us immensely accepting of the need to struggle. "If we do not struggle, we feel almost as though we will not have deserved our success," as Neeti Sharma, a 27-year-old PR professional from Lucknow working in Mumbai puts it. The willingness to struggle is inherent to how we view ourselves and our trajectories.

Accessibility of technology and its social platforms means there is no longer any excuse for those who have missed out. In the thralls of these demands, in the arena in which there is no true excuse to not be noticed, the Starving Artist is putting his money into the best phone and phone camera, a 4G network, clothes and being impeccably turned out, made picture perfect with filters, gaining exposure to the current outrage of the day, films, clubs, restaurants, cool groups and drives to side with, from pet adoption to saving Chennai from its floods, so that he may be ready when opportunity may choose to strike. Those entering fields such as media, advertising, fashion, the film industry, and in dance, theatre, music, or even start-up spheres, equipped with an idea, talent and the ambition to make it big, are all around us, preparing to bite the bullet and if need be, starve. It comes with the territory of success. And we may starve, but we are ready.

Between these two, in the glamourisation of a storyboard kind of success and the making of it into a module which young people are pressured to compose and sell their trajectories, the top line and the bottom line of the Starving Artist paradigm is played out.

The Starving Artist Paradigm results from co-opting a trajectory that would, in a non-accelerated age, take a lifetime to unfold with some reliance on luck and sure-footed talent, by those who would rise in an Instagrammable hurry. Opportunities are few and close fast, and the great idea only has a short window in which to thrive. The value of the self as capital investment means optimising its use across a series of ideas to construct a continual success. To achieve this, you must start early, take risks and attempt a variety of things in a very compressed span of time.

In defence of the pursuit of novelty

Everything is sparkling new, and everything has the potential to be. Even boring old money, around since 700 BC, can be Bitcoin today. We are in an age that is discovering a further digital dimension to everything we thought was set in three-dimensional stone. We must go back to the things we thought we knew and rediscover them all and we are doing so with much abandon.

The reasons for this "irrational exuberance", to borrow a term from Alan Greenspan, are multiple. First being that the diminutive pace at which achievement proceeded in the socialist era allowed, by definition of its ideal, for just enough for everyone. Which meant a house, a car, a job, insurance and medical care was sufficient ambition for a lifetime. With access to loans and the projections of future income growth, the average 28-year-old today is capable of buying his own house or car, and is often opting to rent, or use Uber, instead.

No longer is the big bank balance necessarily the insignia of a wise saver, but is rather indicative of the wastefulness of parked money that achieves little for its possessor. The process of investment is not only tied up in real estate, the share market, and equity, but in the idea of wealth creation per se. The wealthiest person today is not he who grabs opportunity, but he who can create them for others.

The birth of the start-up culture and the freelance/consultant way of working have implied to us that an accelerated incubation of ideas, perspective and wealth can be better harnessed by planting it across multiple sources of future growth with variable outcomes, rather than in one plodding trajectory with only one single outcome—a salary with an annual adjustment for inflation. According to Abhijit Bhaduri, author of *Digital Tsunami*, a survey by an executive search firm in India found that less than 12 per cent of respondents had stayed in their current jobs for more than 10 years. According to Deloitte's annual Millennial Survey in India, two-thirds of the respondents expressed a desire to leave their organisations by 2020 and their main motivations were opportunities to progress and lead. The next shift within India, Bhaduri predicts, will be the shift from career to career—career hopping and not mere job hopping within the parameters of a single career. This births the consultant module. He boils this down to four key factors: a rapid obsolescence of skills, hyper automation, an abundance of career options and the legitimacy of leisure.

Which is why you will often hear the emerging generation employ the phrase, 'it's not about the money'. It's not. It's about what the money has the potential to achieve. Never before has money been so all-consuming, and yet so unimportant, in an essentially consumerist society.

As Indian Prime Minister Narendra Modi put it at the G20 summit in 2016, "There was a time when development was believed to depend on the quantity of labour and capital. Today we know that it depends as much on the quality of institutions and ideas."

Guy Standing speaks of a generation moving in and out of jobs that hold little meaning for them, dubbing them 'The Precariat'. However, Standing calls them 'the new dangerous class', pointing to their precariousness without job security, long-term stability, social protection, and fixed occupational identities in migrant or local labour. When a man no longer acquires his identity from his occupation, Standing believes, he is open to and susceptible to the exploitation of those seeking to co-opt his mutable identity to further their ends, from terrorist groups to those looking to wage ethnic warfare.

"The Precariat lacks occupational identity, even if some have vocational qualifications and even if many have jobs with fancy titles. For some, there is a freedom in having no moral or behavioural commitments that would define an occupational identity. We will consider the image of the 'urban nomad' later, and the related one of 'denizen', the person who is not a full citizen. Just as some prefer to be nomadic, travellers not settlers, so not all those in the Precariat should be regarded as victims. Nevertheless, most will be uncomfortable in their insecurity, without a reasonable prospect of escape."

However, Standing concludes, due to the possible outcomes of vulnerability, this shift in an emerging generation is a negative one. That it is a subconscious product of its age.

Except, it is not. The Precariat is intensely conscious of its choices. It volunteers to set itself on the edge and measure its fall on the way down, hopefully inventing a parachute as it goes. It gains not just its thrills from the dive, but throws itself into the one-on-one discovery of the gaps it can find solutions for. Thus, the entrepreneur believes his personal struggle is an integral part of the solutions he is seeking. And if he will want them, so will others. It is not so much the Precariat as the Explorer of a new age, cutting himself into dense jungles of sociological experience to uncover new ways to develop already-charted territory.

Thus, the stories most start-ups craft today originate in personal lacuna, in the self identity of the founder with the need the company fulfils. From the ill-famed Theranos, which was born out of founder Elizabeth Holmes' fear of needle pricks, to the $1.3bn Airbnb's Joe Gebbia and Brian Chesky, who decided to rent out three rooms in their home in order to make money one month when they were short of their rent. Closer home, Urban Ladder founders Ashish Goel and Rajiv

Srivatsa, built the start-up on their need for an online rental when shopping to furnish their own home, and Zomato was built on Deepinder Goyal and Pankaj Chaddah's visit to the Ambience Mall in Gurgaon for lunch. From Silicon Valley to Bengaluru, the standard has been set—the narrative of a personal story, however big or small, behind every successful start-up has been standardised, and is the watermark of an idea that fits the module of what constitutes modern-day success. It sows the seed that success begins with the story of the self. In the struggle of the 'I' is the seed of the success of the 'I'.

The sum of all this, the novelty of the age, the range of unmapped opportunity and possibility, and the presence of the 'I' in every story of success, is creating a variety of risk takers who craft their thrills occupationally.

A generation of cliff jumpers

Studies by neuropsychiatrist Valerie Voon at the University of Cambridge show that both the ability to binge drink or sky dive and the ability to anticipate risk, are associated with increase in activity in the brain's dopamine regions. Ironically, she points out, this is at once behaviour that seeks reward, but also, the investment in safety mechanisms while taking the risk, stems from an urge to avoid loss. "The likelihood of a thrill from base jumping or a roller coaster is close to 100 per cent. But while the likelihood of death from a roller coaster ride is 0 per cent, the chances of dying from base jumping are considerably higher. The closer to the extremes, 0 per cent or 100 per cent, the more certain, whereas the closer to 50 per cent, the more uncertain...", she writes, going on to explain that people with a certain dopamine receptor seek greater responses to unexpected rewards, from unexpected thrills. In as much as it is a brain function, it is also a function of upbringing and environment and peer pressure, which is why adolescents are typically more thrill-seeking than adults. Voon's studies and experiments with asking participants to choose from a series of faces, what would make for risky gambles or safe choices, indicating that novelty, a range of options, increases dopamine release, which enhances the expectation of reward.

With the rising range of options then, a young generation is not entirely risk averse. It believes that rewards may be higher, and is game for exploration. With reference to Nobel-Prize winning psychologist Daniel Kahneman's Prospect Theory in which 'losses loom larger than gains', Dr Heidi Grant Halvorson, Associate Director of the Motivation Science Centre at Columbia University, says that we only actually choose that option when the stability maintains a status quo of gains ('The Hidden Danger of Being Risk Averse', *Harvard Business Review*, July 02, 2013). This understanding is an outcome of 20 years of research at the University by Tony Higgins, who calls this counter theory 'Prevention Focus'. He explains it as "a robust aversion to being wide-eyed and optimistic, making mistakes, and taking chances." The rest of us are 'promotion-focused', choosing risk when it holds potential for rich gains. Studies at the Columbia Motivation Science Centre show the prevention-focussed as working more deliberately and slowly, seeking reliability over 'coolness' or luxury in products, and preferring conservative investments to high yielding but less certain ones. So while Alan Greenspan blamed the recent recession on 'irrational exuberance', or too much risk taking, Halvorson notes that those who took risks at the time may not actually be the ones at fault. This is because prevention focus only actually works when the going is good. When risk is required, to prevent loss, those averse to risk are not capable of making the leap. However, in order to return to status quo, they often take a harder risk than they are used to or comprehend. This leads to them making riskier risks, as opposed to the calculated risks of the serial risk taker, out of desperation rather than understanding of the outcome. She cites the example of Bruno Iksil, JP Morgan's 'London whale', who doubled down on a losing bet rather than admit his losses, ultimately costing the bank over 6 million pounds; she explains his actions were not born of over confidence, but desperation. From the vantage point of the traditionalist, the conservative, risk, then, is just what you take when things don't work out, and when you need them to return to status quo. However, for the non-traditionalist, risk is an ongoing investment and the sum of his past gambles, won or failed at, which contribute to his skill at wielding a final Big Risk outcome. This is also born out by SEBI's NCAER Survey of How Households Save and Invest, 2011, which stated: "In case of windfall gains, households with low level of assets engaged in risky behaviour (participated in the derivative market) compared to households that own progressively higher level of assets." Risk behaviour patterns in India, affected by budget constraints and liquidity and income, broadly indicate that the more educated, the younger and the more urban the person, the more risk-prone he or she is, even as investments in traditional asset classes, like real estate and gold, for that age group and demographic are declining.

Ergo, unlike the generation before, with a wide variety of ideas and careers that have the potential to bring windfall games, it chooses a radical precariousness not with uncertainty, but with a certainty of the risks it embraces, and it correspondingly expects proportionate rewards for it. The only difference being those who were always risk-friendly take more calculated risks, and the traditionally risk-averse are now flinging themselves off the riskier risk cliffs. Both want the outcome of promised windfall gains. Some get them, some do not. Whichever may land on his or her feet, the investment in risk per se is clear.

Poster boys of risk

More than a 'Precariat' then replacing a Proletariat, it is rather the 'Riskeoisie' taking over from the Bourgeoisie, making a capital investment in the experiential gamble.

As if in an ingenious reversal to the unfair sharing of property, capital and resources, it is as though the individual stepped up to take charge, and said "No more will I invest in making you richer. From now, I make me richer". In the self-aggrandising individual, thus, Proletariat and Precariat and Bourgeoisie meet. The risk taker now immerses himself in the qualitative physicality of achievement. The being present in the story. Which is why you also now have to 'Instagram it, or it didn't happen'. The presence is bigger than the experience.

When the investment is in risk, and not in its outcome, the capital becomes the risk taker, or the founder, or the holder of the idea. Which is why the idea may change, and a founder of one company will typically jump to another, and then another.

The poster boy of the Riskeoisie is Elon Musk. You have to gamble big and dream big to believe in making transport space age, but for a certain generation, nothing less than the moon will do. Musk may have begun with Zip2, but must roll that ability for hedging his bets into a SpaceX, a Tesla, and a Hyperloop, and other ideas which may well fail, but which contribute to his overall success. No single failure becomes his overwhelming failure. No single success is sufficient success. Because the capital is not the outcome, it is his Riskeoisie, which is now both his asset class, what he owns, and because this is himself, he also acquires the characteristics of owning it. And the measure of each of us is how Riskoisie we are and how long and how well we sustain by it.

After having gained this vibrato of employability, the freedom of exploration that comes from a range, the identity that comes from stability, hitting just one or a few notes, is unpalatable and restrictive. On the contrary, the occupation today gains its identity from its founders and employees. While the Precariat rues the loss of occupational identity, the Riskoeisie welcomes it.

The resultant brand building is what education strategist Meeta Sengupta identifies as the Individual 'NPV' or the Net

Present Value. While organisations calculate the difference between present cash inflows and outflows in order to calculate the profitability of a projected investment, individuals are now calculating NPVs for themselves. So, when you spend out of your pocket to buy things that are seemingly frivolous, from an expensive haircut to branded shoes, in order to impress a boss, teammates, fit into a work culture, acquire a signature 'look', the mental calculation, knowingly or unknowingly, or even an expensive educational course that one has taken out a loan for, all goes towards the assessment of an Individual NPV.

This is because the investment is not in one's career or in the company one works for. It is in the all-too visible self-identity. Consequently, it is Brand 'I' that gains the financial, emotional and social investment, and all its associated risks. But it is Brand 'I' that will be carried from success to success and failure to failure. The trap, as with the prevention-focussed, is when the risk is not consciously taken, assessed, or willing, and when the brand building is a non-strategic by-product of peer pressure and social forces.

The Precariat can be identified by a distinctive structure of social income, which imparts a vulnerability going well beyond what would be conveyed by the money income received at a particular moment. For instance, in a period of rapid commercialisation of the economy of a developing country, the new groups, many going towards the Precariat, find that they lose traditional community benefits and do not gain enterprise or state benefits. They are more vulnerable than many with lower incomes who retain traditional forms of community support as well as salaried employees who have similar money incomes but have access to an array of enterprise and state benefits. A feature of the Precariat is not the level of money wages or income earned at any particular moment but the lack of community support in times of need, lack of assured enterprise or state benefits, and lack of private benefits to supplement money earnings.

"We are in an era of the legitimacy of leisure"

Abhijit Bhaduri, Digital Transformation Coach and Author of *Digital Tsunami*

It's not about classifying this generation as millennial, or Generation X, Y, S. These are largely misnomers because in India, the big shift came with liberalisation. Consequently, we have only two kinds of generations – the pre-liberalisation and the post-liberalisation ones.

For the larger part, this is the first generation that doesn't need to support their parents, or send money home unlike the previous generations where whoever started working first took on the cost of supporting a large network of people. Kids today do have disposable income. So they are able to take risks. Emotional and financial security lends them a cushion. The previous era was also one which looked at leisure as a sin. Today, it is not so. At a workplace, a fresher is unlikely to shut the browser tab on which he is checking his Facebook because his boss showed up whereas the generation before pretended to work even if they had none. That was what was done – you looked busy. Today, I don't have to explain to you why I relax.

There is search for meaning in a job, not merely an income. So few have qualms about quitting. We've moved from a scarcity mentality to an abundance mentality.

In the age where there are 5 million self-employed, the young person is constantly asking how he can differentiate himself. Social media becomes a huge driver of that. The fear that nobody will want to hire you is diminished. I know someone who quit their job to train dogs and who supplements the loss of the full-time job with training, writing columns for newspapers and is very happy without the notional identity lent by occupation. Effectively, what young people are doing today is building their own brand.

Where earlier individuals were known by the organisations they worked for, today organisations come to be known by the individuals who work for them. When Deloitte bought Josh Bersin, it didn't become a Deloitte company, but 'Bersin by Deloitte'. So also with 'Casey Quirk by Deloitte'. The roles have switched and the *individual becomes the most important asset the company can have and becomes a brand unto himself. The consumer owns your brand, thus establishing the supremacy of the peer economy.*

♦ ♦ ♦

Brand 'I', the individual unit of this economy, is both what drives it and falls victim to it, all at once sustainer and destroyer of itself.

Section IV
Go for Broke

Rentals & Freebies - Financial Literacy

₹13.

Rentals and Freebies

The stupid things that you do because you think that poor is cool Pulp

"There's a point where everyone turns religious"

Shridhar Ahuja, 29, Financial Analyst, London

When you travel overseas for higher studies, most people think 'that guy has it made'. But the thing is most of us have come from middle class families, we have applied for scholarships, our parents have sold something or the other for the flight ticket – a house if they have it or gold at the very least, borrowed money temporarily to put into the account to show a balance so you'll get the visa – and you've had to buy the 'basics' which are actually quite expensive, from warm clothes to that laptop on student discount. So once you are here, there is very little leeway. You have to make it. You shut up and put up and get through whatever you don't have. The commute, buses, subways, everything adds up when you are in a country where even water costs money. The first step of compromise is food. It is not uncommon for many graduate students on scholarships to survive without meals for two to three days at a time. The most common excuse is that they are not able to adjust to the foreign kind of food, and they miss home, but in reality, they don't have the spare change. One of the things that makes the biggest difference is the local gurudwara or Ramakrishna Mission or temple that gives out prasad and langar. For me, it was the Havelock Road Temple, Gurudwara in West London. You can't imagine what a boon that is for those of us who have gone without.

There have been days when I was a student when that was my only meal a day. For that alone, I believe in God.

♦♦♦

How to game the system

The lack of subversion—of what is cool, of what is standardised, of what is mainstream—in popular culture, unlike the generation of a decade ago, means that today's crowd gravitates towards establishment. If coffee house culture is cool, the migrant culture, today, takes the symbols of mass culture that are hitting the popularity charts as a public inscribing of themselves with success. So, wanting to be seen in the Starbucks over the *thela*, or the use of high street brands like Zara or Marks & Spencers and standing in queue for the opening of H&M, is not only a desire to acquire the status that wearing those brands lends one, but it speaks of contributing to and participating in the win those indicators speak of, and performs a self-evaluation of where amongst the peer group one ranks. The need to fit into the mainstream also comes from a very practical mindset—in an era of mass, which usually means the wholesale, the overarching e-platforms that offer sales and discounts, conformity to the mass has begun to mean the ability to fit into a larger, more global framework of employment and education opportunity. As the world grows more homogeneous, it is necessary to fit in, not stand out, in order to sneak oneself an advantage. The paradox of the modern age is the need to stand out, while yet fitting in.

Belonging, finding one's tribe is as integral to the process of growing up and finding one's role in society as hitting those social milestones—graduation, employment, marriage, kids, buying a house and so on and so forth. It is an almost instinctive process and is of as much psychological value to well-being as is physical health. This is why, in migratory settlements across the globe, not just in India, people travelled together and lived in close communion with each other. Hence, you have the Southall Indians in the UK, or the Jackson Heights (as one businessman quipped, 'also fondly known as Jai Kishen Heights'), Chinatowns, so on and so forth.

This community bonding fulfills the very tribal urge of safety, especially for migrants, but it also fulfills very tangible economic needs. The procurement of a kind of food grain, pulse, spice, the comfort of eating by hand, or even knowing what to order, and the familiarity of the mother tongue are made collective, the cost comes down and scant resources are shared—these are all unquantifiable cadences of the migratory spirit that only begin to hit home when you are walking down a wintry road in Manhattan and someone calls out in Hindi asking if you'd like some chai. It is an inexplicable lighting up even for the least territorial of us. I distinctly recall that in the 1980s, as emigrants to Lagos, Nigeria, the entire expat community, my parents included, at dinner or an evening out at the World Trade Centre, would stop what they were doing and run to the window to cheer and applaud if a Sardarji on a Bajaj scooter rolled by on the street outside. I never knew why we were applauding but it just seemed like such a joyful thing to do, to identify with this unknown man on a strange inexpensive looking vehicle on a foreign road just because he connected us in some small way to a sense of home. This is tribal instinct. More importantly, it bolsters the community and those within it who do not have the ability to fend for themselves.

In a society where opening out education systems encourage white-collar migration patterns to move towards occupational movement rather than community movement, the idea that the individual must now fend for himself, is ingrained. As more and more urban societies are composed of these migrants, the tribe, as it were, is formed by indicators other than language, community, food or religion. In this transition period, those who cling to these older indicators are left behind, and those who do not adapt to the new, are in danger of being so too.

Increasingly, the new indicators are set by the workplace, by the media, and by popular culture.

These now get defined by different parameters. These could be the clothes one buys and aspires to, brands one uses to define one's personality type—such as the Enfield Bullet, by places one is seen to frequent—such as bars or clubs, or holiday destinations, by commonality of exposure—to books, to hobbies and interests, by travel, and even by associations from one's past such as alumni, or sporting clubs, runner's groups etc. With the broadening of these markers of who one is, and what tribe one belongs to, it becomes necessary to invest in these circuits to achieve a mental and physical sense of belonging.

Where it sometimes gets blown out of proportion is when the media uses clues from pop culture, more film stars and rock stars, or even the vacuous celebrity-for-no-earthly-reason as clothes horses for the advocacy of this new age tribalism. Endorsements at this level involve big money, aspirational spending, and entire corporate structures whose survival depends on a particular look, style, feel and brand being adapted as the identifying marker of a tribe, any tribe will do, but it is mostly the tribe of the impressionable young that is sought to be tapped.

This is the cauldron out of which a culture of keeping up begins to bubble and toil. But it is also out of this self-same cauldron, a churning of the ocean that elicits both the good and the poison out of the self-same expanse, that young people are finding solutions.

One of them is the emerging market for rentals.

"Contrary to popular opinion, the new generation is smart, not dumb, in how they negotiate spending. An older generation was too caught up in issues of caste and class and social snobbery to even consider renting clothes for one specific occasion. Today's generation has absolutely no qualms," points out Radhika Bansal, co-founder of Swishlist, an apparel rental service. It is also, contrary to popular opinion, culturally something we are comfortable with. We are a society that borrows saris, hand-me downs from our siblings and cousins, or a ghaghra from an aunt. We do have a conscious sense of what constitutes wasteful expenditure, while keeping in mind social impressions.

For Bansal, 35, and Vedika Oberoi, 32, founders of Swishlist, epiphany came when they had a couple of weddings in a single month three years ago and found themselves having to buy 15 outfits, and that too for someone else's wedding. "There is today immense pressure to keep up. With so much of celebrity styling, people are keeping track of trends, they know what make-up is in, which designers are doing what, what's showing at fashion week, which brand names are cool. These are not all higher income groups, a majority of our customers are from the middle income groups, from working women to housewives. Also with the age of social media, Instagram, Facebook and Snapchat, so many people are taking selfies and uploading stuff that it becomes difficult to repeat an outfit. People are watching and people want to be seen. So how do you keep up?" With icons like Ranveer Singh or Virat Kohli trying to set new trends in fashion on a cyclical basis to further their own lines of merchandise or endorsements, the impact is on men as much as women.

Rentals become a great option for a young generation of migrants because most of them lead active social lives that revolve around people they don't really know that well. Heavier investments, lifetime investments in owning things, jewellery, clothes, brands, come when commitments mature, when one is vested in that relationship. Given the pace of fragmentary relationships, and constantly moving circuits, networks that function on multiple dimensions, it doesn't make sense to invest in appearance beyond a point. The fleeting rental serves the purpose brilliantly.

"They are at an age when someone is getting married or engaged, someone is having a party, and they are young, outgoing, and dating. They also believe that since they work hard for their money they deserve to indulge themselves as they don't have any other immediate responsibilities. It's easy to say this is not how an older generation spent their money but the driving forces today are different. It is not just that we can't afford to buy that expensive *anarkali* to wear to a friend's wedding, not even your own sister's—when it is a family wedding, you have a budget, when it is a friend, you don't have a separate budget for the *sangeet* and for the main ceremony, but it still means a lot to you, so you want to go well dressed." Another problem her customers posit is that for Indian wear you can still get a tailor to make it for you at a cheaper cost, but for western or fusion wear, which is in fashion, there are no cost-effective alternatives. If you don't buy a good quality designer, it shows up badly in fit or material and cut. So when the dress code is formal Western or fusion, a trend sometimes enforced by peer pressure, there is no option but to pick an expensive option.

Aboli Salvi began Sharewardrobe in New Delhi when she returned from the US and found that there was only so much space, and the winter wardrobe would have to go when summer came. The first year, she gave away the clothes to the colony maids, who accumulated them, in pristine condition, expensive and suited for other weathers and countries, and distributed them, cocktail dresses and skirts, tops and gowns, not to wear, but to rip up into sections to make into patchwork rugs. Her heart broke. Resolving never to have to go through that again, she realised there must surely be others with good clothes that are just getting thrown away. Sharewardrobe began in order to be able to recycle those clothes. Salvi's biggest concern she says was that her customers would find the second-hand nature of clothes taboo. But she quickly realised the issue was not that they would be second-hand, but that they would look second-hand and would not be hygienic. Once those two aspects were taken care of, they were good to go. Clothes pass stringent quality checks, are dry cleaned, and the option of second-hand with tags are also available for picky customers. Today she has over 4,000 members, mostly from Delhi. "It's not just about not being able to afford something, but there's also the issue of not wanting to put money aside for it. Several working women need a particular formal cocktail dress for just one night, could be a formal company party, annual dinner, awards function and they know they will not use that dress again, so why bother with the expense." Salvi believes women are more cautious of spending money than men though many men also call her to procure outfits and accessories for their wives. In accessories, it's designer bags that go cheaper.

Several such sites now exist across metros, from Flyrobe to Wrapd, Liberent and Klozee. Many get one level smarter. Why rent at all? When clothing wear e-sites first launched, many inspired by the American model offered a no-questions-asked return policy. "Several young people would order the clothes for the weekend, wear it with the label cleverly removed or tucked in so as not to be visible, and return it on Monday, and we would be obliged to return the money", an Amazon executive said on condition of anonymity. The practice extended to mobile phones as well, pushing Amazon Fulfilled to pull the return policy as the company was ending up with bearing the restocking fee and the shipping fee. The returns policy has raised several seller hackles and has been an ongoing issue with sites like Myntra, Flipkart and others who sell online. Sujayath Ali at Voonik says they combat the issue by focusing on tier 2 and 3 towns, where goods take longer to arrive by courier, cutting the possibility of frivolous deliveries by a substantial amount.

But sellers are really in no position to grumble. The penchant for rentals, the use-and-throw phenomenon, is a by-product of the 'buy now pay later' and everything-is-dispensable economy that these kind of start-ups need to build in order to find sellers for their own products. An environment of transience is ingrained in the entire consumer culture both corporates and the consumers who feed off and feed into them, are cohabiting. There is no one without another.

Life hacks from a proud Dubai mooch

Ronnie Joseph, 27, Dubai

My *parents are well-accomplished government servants (the ones with no access to black money, I should add) and I am their only child—an engineer and an MBA from tier 1 colleges, both of which were paid for by my parents. For which I am thankful. That puts me as somewhat a stereotype of a so-called ideal Indian career path (which I truly detest).*

Avoiding debt in Dubai is not easy when debt is cheap and slavery is cheaper. I was placed in a firm which paid me well, but not as well as my peers who were placed in another company there.

For the first six months or so, I lived in a cheaper part of town near my workplace and the airport with strangers I was not comfortable with, riding the bus or the metro to visit my friends on weekends. I often walked down to office two kilometres away and counted everything I bought from the supermarket. Going for the cheapest cereal so that I won't have to splurge for breakfast at the cafeteria, counting every dirham spent every day.

Using a basic Nokia phone was the best feeling those days, away from the clutter of social media notifications and annoyance of charging it daily. Since I was on training most of the time I could afford to do so as there would not be any client mails I had to attend to. Also, I had faith in my friends to still be there without being constantly in touch with them. At this point, I used to be able to save at least 40 per cent of my salary, though 25 per cent was my target every month, which I meticulously set aside as un-spendable.

You Only Live Once

At the end of six months, I could afford to pay for my overpriced Driver's License and got it in my third attempt (depleted almost Rs 1 lakh on it). But I chose to do it in February for two reasons. The month was shorter so my cash flow cycle was reduced (even few days counted), also summer was coming and I needed to have it before then, as my job involved travelling for meetings, and I was hell-bent on not spiralling into debt, and never for a depreciating asset for that matter. I decided to go for a second-hand car with all my savings. This was when I committed the gravest error in judgement: To buy an old Jaguar off of a Ugandan without due diligence (talk about penny wise, pound foolish). It was a hit among my friends though and by this time I had moved in with them in the better locality. A painful 30 days later, I had systems failing left, right and centre. The last straw was the AC. I sold it back to the same person at a little loss. That was the day I could sleep well for the first time in 30 days. How bad could my luck be? I thought.

I now had most of my savings back and it was almost the month end. First thing I did was introduce myself to the joys of renting. Although it was a Chevy Cruz, it was new, and most importantly, I didn't own it. I could go on about my various adventures, beating loopholes in renting, and borrowing colleagues' cars during their annual leaves.

I developed an entire cheat sheet of mooching and sharing by focusing on what was important to me.

I continued to live in a nice hotel apartment with my friends for the rest of my time in that country. But I lived out of a suitcase for two years, with exactly five pairs of formal shirts, a few t-shirts and one pair of jeans, one pair of formal shoes, one pair of sandals. Slippers, I borrowed. Sometimes, people called me cheap but then realised I was proud of it rather than ashamed of it.

While my friends were paying down payments and buying Land Cruisers and BMWs and being liable for the next five years, I never had such a long term plan there, so I was renting a lowly hatch most of the time which did the job, and hey, I could drive the others whenever I wanted.

I always ran my personal finances like a listed company, calculating my liquidity every week and whether I met the mark in terms of savings and where I could waste less. I spent most of my weekends working on my pet projects, rather than go out and blow money up on alcohol. I say most, as I did indulge in it once a month at least so as to be part of the memories that were created.

Most of the social time I spent in cooking with friend on weekends, helping them out with groceries, hopping in with them to the car wash or for a walk. The kind of things where you don't end up spending money.

Always looking for ways to earn an extra buck. Had friends in electronics industry, so this once, I got three drones for 300 a piece and sold them online for 800 a piece. I would use my credit card to pay the hotel apartment rent for two to three flats, which I claimed in cash and deposited same day to earn points and redeem coupons. My biggest asset was the positive relations I had built in those times which helped me to borrow things from friends who trusted me and to get inside deals in the industries they worked in (maybe concert passes, free fishing trips by their suppliers and goodies, as well as information on sales and offers before they were made public).

I am now back in India with a voluntary 70 per cent pay cut which I took to be part of the start-up culture here. I am more content than ever. I live in tier 2 cities or the outskirts. I've travelled far and wide in my dad's 11-year-old car, which I resurrected from death. Living like a nomad, still living out of the same suitcase (now I have to hand wash instead of using the washing machine!).

Most important to me was paying back my Dad the Rs 10 lakh he paid for my education, without him asking for it. The best education I had was the one trying to make it back.

I will probably not buy a car soon and will still keep using hand-me-down phones and things. In the end, I realised you don't have to pretend or live beyond your means when you have built meaningful relations who accept you for who you are and you accept them for who they are and that never changes. You clearly know what you can afford and what you can avoid. Also, you are open to learning and growing wiser every year.

♦♦♦

Financial Literacy

Everything's gonna be fine fine fine 'cause I've got one hand in my pocket And the other one is giving a high five Alanis Morisette

I'm 40, and as I write this, my EMI cheques will bounce tomorrow not because I don't have a job, or don't have an income, but because my EMIs come first and the salary comes later and they are in two different banks, and I haven't yet figured out how to sync the two. If you don't have financial literacy, no matter how much money you have, your personal balance sheet will always be in the red. I've also never had the money to do the things I actually wanted to do in life — like visit that Wassily Kandinsky exhibit at the Louvre, or trek New Zealand from tip to tip that I still have the brochures for from after graduation. But this is because I took a lot of loans to do spur of the moment things — like that mad do-everything-you-want weekend I'd devised for my son at Fort Aguada in Goa, or his first iPad — but which you end up paying for through the next five years, in instalments. My mother pledged her gold ornaments to help me put a down payment on the house I bought. I couldn't return the amount in time and they were gone. I have a small fund that I put money into to try to return that amount, but the truth of finance is, it builds up much slower than it diminishes. Determined to clean up, I once went to a financial planner in Vashi who was recommended by an astute business journalist friend who seemed to have it all sorted, but he kept listing my loans and asking me what I was going to pay them with. I told him that if I'd known, I wouldn't need him.

Financial literacy is like dieting: It is very possible to either overeat or starve, and both do very little to alter the actual fat-to-muscle ratio of the body, mainly because we have not understood how the body works. Most of us comprehend this because we can see the tangible outcomes of dieting, albeit in terms of cloth sizes on the rack, how we look in selfies and photographs, and in the every day feedback of people. They say this post-liberalisation generation is self-obsessed but it does more—it looks at itself with a clear eye and it is unafraid of what it sees. The Photoshop generation was in the 1990s. Today's puts itself up on a Facebook post, for better or for worse, and takes a whole lot of personal comments on the chin. It reads its flaws and shortfalls well. The reason they are not able to do this with financial information, is because unlike the state of the body, the financial red is kept hidden.

The Internet and financial planning websites, newspapers and magazines galore will tell you how to read interest rates on credit cards, personal loans, the importance of saving 10 per cent of your income, blah blah blah. It's all out there in every format from video to Buzzfeed listicle. The Google generation doesn't need one more exercise in how to save money. What it needs is to understand why those tools and that information are powerless to move their bank balances upwards. Here is a five-point plan to taking control of a financial predicament that has less to do with money, and more with grappling with why we mess our finances up in the first place/repeatedly.

1. Lift the curtain of silence

The first ask of financial literacy is to put it out there. Confess. Put it down in black and white where it is visible. Not in the public domain—you don't owe random strangers your truth, unless you feel that that will hold you accountable and you want to do that voluntarily —not in spaces that will make you vulnerable, but perhaps with a trusted friend, a relative, parents, anyone who loves you and whose withering eye will be tough to take, but necessary for your future growth. Most case studies in this book are of people quietly dealing with their financial troubles alone. This is the first time they've spoken, and several said to me: "Please use my real name, I'm tired of pretending."

It's something that George Orwell also nods to in his aforementioned treatise, *Down and Out in Paris and London*, on being broke: "It is a feeling of relief, almost of pleasure, at knowing yourself at last genuinely down and out. You have talked so often of going to the dogs—and well, here are the dogs, and you have reached them, and you can stand it. It takes off a lot of anxiety."

There are many ways in which to achieve financial literacy. A financial planner is one, but most of those work for when you have money to apportion to one need or another.

The first thing to do is to list your income—all your income, and your outflow—all of it, even the cashless, credit, automated, the Rs 10 chocolate you bought at the train station on the way to work and the flight ticket home that Dad bought. Put it down. Make it tangible, visible, the way your company does when it hands you your offer letter—what is your break-up per month, and per year. Look at the totals of both and put the figures up somewhere you can see them, a pin board, tacked to the fridge, on your phone screen saver. The difference between the two is the gap you need to fill to live comfortably. If you earn Rs 10 and spend Rs 18, you need to write down that Rs 8 in big bold letters somewhere where it hits you.

2. Know your priorities. Your priorities are not others' priorities.

The second thing to do is to see how you want to fix it. Do you want to increase your income to cover the Rs 8? Or reduce your expense? The answer may seem simple enough to many, but it isn't so for those living it. You cannot arrive at this answer until you pin down what is important to you.

One of the major problems young people have in taking advice from the previous generation, which believes it has all the financial answers, is that several do not see as 'necessity' what the current generation does. So, it goes through the list of expenses and says "Clubbing? Remove. Eating out? Remove. Uber? Remove..." etc. Except, none of those are realistic to a 24-year-old whose peer pressures drive him to participate in a highly visible and vibrant economy. When you tell him to remove it, he will remove it from your visible presence. It then gets recycled back to being a hidden expense that corrodes quietly and over time into financial health. So often, a financial planner is not the second step.

The second step is to understand why those expenses are important to the person putting in so much money towards dealing with them. If you looked at the expense statement of a person below the age of 30, you have a good idea of what their priorities are in life.

In as much, it makes more sense to seek the help of a therapist, a counsellor, or someone in your personal space who performs that role for you, rather than a financial planner. Without understanding oneself, there is no balance sheet that can clear the debt.

The lens applied is typically one of judgement, but change the lens, and empathy elicits very different answers. A Rs 10,000 bill at Zara says 'I need X (a boss, friend circle, the people I share a home with) to think better of me'. Who is the person whose approval is sought? What is the fear driving that need for approval? And will shifting out of that environment help? An expensive gym membership might be what keeps you going mentally and physically when everything else around you is failing. Don't cut it out because someone else thinks it's not important. Make a priority list of what is vital to *you*.

At the same time, knock your investment until it responds to the hard questions: Is there a cheaper way to do this? Can I sign up for the marathon and train on the roads with a running group instead? Will I make friends that share my fitness goals and get that side of me *and* manage to save money?

With some, it is the need to make it and be visible in that industry, in which case, treat the investment in personal image as a professional expense. But then question if the clothes and accessories—props to the con essentially—one is buying are classics, long lasting and contributing to the larger required image. Can these be rented? Shared with a friend? You will find some of them non-negotiable, and others are. Pick solutions for whatever is negotiable. Fashion blogs often offer good tips on shopping cheap, DIY and what constitute classics even in a haute couture obsessed world. Sites like Voonik help you tweak your tastes so you're buying better, and not just more. Ask a stylist, friend or professional, for tips. A one-time payment on good advice might save you thousands in the long run. There are many ways to improve the quality of that investment, while nipping and tucking a bit here and there.

For others, it's being held to impossible standards by a boss or superior who holds the employee to outwardly exhibitions of class no matter what the quality of work put in. Have a discussion, first with friends, and if required with the superior, on either holding your own, dressing as you feel comfortable within the framework of the existing dress code, or changing your workplace. Sometimes, you'll realise the senior didn't realise they were beating down on you for what you perceive as a personal standard of dressing. Ask the question: Is how one dresses more or as important than the work they do? If the answer is 'yes', ask why, and you'll probably get either the need for that job profile to appear well dressed or find a response that shows you how shallow the space you work in is. Then you'll know what to do.

Much of the shaming is real, it's public, and it exists across levels from junior to senior-most, no matter what the income level. Hence, it's not so simple as to advise young people up financial red creek to 'withstand peer pressure'.

Sometimes, it's about investing in right things in order to keep up appearances, rise in the job, and achieve the next level of success as well.

A good idea is to make yourself a personal balance sheet of where you want to be, in terms of personal and professional roles, in the next five years. Then list the things you spend on (not their cost) in the debit and the credit sections. What's keeping you from your goals, and what's getting you there? Then you'll know what you can eliminate. For example, if you answer 'peak fitness' in a goal, then 'drinking sessions with buddies' goes in the debit for the calories, and not the cost. When you remove what's not important to you, the accompanying cost will be eliminated. If you want to apply for a prestigious fellowship in an American university as a goal, but aren't doing so because of lack of time to study for it, the partying and hang out sessions become a debit to your goal, and not just a cost. Then ask yourself if it's worth it. If it still is, then by all means, either ask yourself why, what they feed you — would a study group with a shared common goal fortify your need for 'some company', if that's the answer you are left with? If not, see if you need to reconsider your goals.

For yet others, it's personal. It's a boyfriend one needs to impress or a circuit of friends who always have more money than one does. The question one needs to begin with is why those people, in particular, comprise your social circuit. Did they happen to be the first people you made friends with? Are they just colleagues, former and new? Habit? Are you living in an area in which these just happen to be handy? Or do you genuinely like them? Do you aspire to be like them? In the life hack work flow, there are solutions to each of these. Perhaps it's time to identify and find your own tribe.

The trick is to know oneself, what one's own priorities are, and what the instruments of non-negotiable social and professional currency are in your own line of work and find solutions within that framework. There is no one answer for all.

Only when you have an understanding of what drives you to make the purchases that you do make, will you be able to resolve actually making them.

For me, it's simple. My son will leave home after his 12th standard so I want him to have as good a time in the now — books, clothes, travel and experiences of life. I have plenty of time to save later. So I spend more than I should possibly afford on the things that seem frivolous to many. To me, however, the investment is in my son's future understanding of life — what I leave him with in terms of exposure to the world, taste, and aesthetics. I compromise on everything else. For instance, I still do not have kitchen cabinets four years after moving into my own home, and so I do not call friends over for dinners or lunches, because my house looks half-done and shabby. Could I achieve that in a couple of months if I saved up? Quite possibly. However, that's a pay-off I'm willing to make. And besides, how would I know which friends and colleagues are willing to just accept my half-built home? I also use my inadequacies to measure others and what I mean to them, as much as I use them to know what they mean to me.

So, pick your own pay-offs and pay them off. You owe no explanations about what you are willing to make compromises for.

3. Pick one: reduce expense or increase income.

The previous understanding is what will lead you to the third step. Understand that it is imperative for your own progress to pick one of the two. Go up, or go down. Once you know what is non-negotiable for you, you will know what that final figure is that you need to make up between income and expense — what is your personal Rs 8?

The first question this begets is: is your job paying you what you are worth? The answer comes as much from a sense of self-worth as from the fact of your material needs being met. If the answer is 'no', then ask yourself why you are still in it. It could be that the job pays really badly, but you remain out of a sense of loyalty. Perhaps the job fulfils your social needs. Perhaps you are gaining valuable work experience on it that compensates for the lack of income because it will propel you into a different league afterwards.

According to the Deloitte Millenial Survey, 2016, 66 per cent of millennials are preparing to leave their jobs in the next one year. By the year 2020, two out of every three people who currently form your immediate work environment will have left to seek opportunities that fulfil their goals. What of yours?

Should you decide to increase your income, there are two ways to do it. One is to plan for and find a job that pays you better. If you are stuck in an industry where market forces keep the pay low, see if there is a part-time job you can do that helps you increase your income.

My dog-walker, Mangesh, is a 26-year-old who walks dogs from 5 AM to 7 AM every morning in half-hour slots that add 12,000 rupees to his income every month. He also claims to enjoy the walking, and it helps that he loves the company of dogs (who wouldn't?).

The era of being ashamed of being spotted getting your hands dirty is long gone. It's the era of pressing your hobbies and passions into paying your way. A friend makes and sells almond milk because she's vegan and knows how to. She has a rollicking home-based side business on weekends. Another is a part-time wedding portfolio photographer. She doesn't do the hired photographer shots, but does those select beautiful pictures that the bride wants to frame for the living room, not the usual tacky candid ones, but artistic and quirky portrayals. A young lady in the housing society I live in has begun yoga classes in her living room. There are a whole lot of micro opportunities flourishing everywhere and if you rack your brains a little bit, there's always a way to make some more money legally, and without violating the terms of your employment contracts.

4. Understand want vs need

To rise in a career framework is possibly a need, to network, is a want. The need is the non-negotiable, the want is often just one way — often the most popular or obvious way — to achieve it. It is, however, not the only way. Nail down your needs, and question your wants, hold them accountable to you and your goals.

I spent many an evening standing in Page 3 parties surrounded by the who's who of Mumbai, clutching a champagne glass, in possibly the hottest parties of that night, making awkward conversation, only to find myself wishing I could just be home with my son. I still do not know over three-fourths of the people in those rooms. I have not made a substantial connection from the investment in networking to shape my career or my writing, let alone my bank balance or my personal life. What I do see as a substantial contribution to my intellectual life, in fact, came from connections I made out of personal interest. I would attend sessions of the P.E.N. chapter when Nissim Ezekiel or Ranjit Hoskote was chairing them. It taught me to enjoy language, appreciate critical thinking, and how to and where to listen to a variety of academic opinions. A few friends made at book readings. A columnist I called up to say how much I enjoyed their column.

When my son was a baby in the crèche, I would have to run back home by 8 PM sharp to pick him up, so I never had a social life. The one I had was limited to a few friends coming home, maybe once or twice a year. To prevent myself from burning out, every few months, I would take an off day at work, leave home at the same time as I would every day for work, and roam the art galleries, more because they were the only places I could go for free. I would then treat myself to a small lunch at a table for one, typically at an Irani restaurant, watch a movie if I could, and catch the regular train home from work. I managed to meet a lot of gallerists, who saw me there in unusually empty hours, and to pose questions to many student and senior artists who would be present in the galleries. Years later, almost a decade later, the information and the knowledge provided a background when I began to write on art. It still doesn't make me an expert, but it makes me a more layered writer in the subject, one who enjoys what she does in her engagement with that subject.

So yes, connections matter, but do they necessarily matter in the way that society says they must be shaped? Deeper connections and more lasting influences emerge from personal initiative and the reaching out we do privately, the follow-ons, more than in the slight nod of the head and a generic smile, while overdressed, in a space where few conversations leave a meaningful impact on either person in the party.

If you must network, do it on terms that build lasting relationships and impact for you.

What do you need to achieve? And what do you want to do to achieve that? One is not a compromise you are willing to make; the other is an interesting way to achieve it. If something in your hands in a store is a want that you are confusing for a need, put it down and walk away.

5. Be yourself

In the end, the clichés all come true. The things they beat you over the head with, when you join a new job or start out in your social circuit, become your virtues as you grow with experience. Anyone with a few years of experience in any field knows this. That stubbornness turns to 'tenacity'. That inability to control your emotions becomes 'highly passionate'. That inability to stick to a job turns to 'wide ranging experience in...' And the woman who kept taking days off to go tend to stray cats ('so unprofessional!') has now become a highly paid animal behaviourist who works out of home. The one who had so little money to dress up for the parties that she actually hand-stitched her own glitter and appliqué patches with needle and thread is today a stylist who works with designer Sabyasachi. Director Anurag Kashyap's life on the street extrapolates into an entire cinematic oeuvre. The inability to find a home translates into an entire start-up equal to the net worth of an Amazon. They'll all tell you, 'you are flawed'. Everyone is. That's what makes them them.

You become, professionally and personally, the sum of your experience of life. At the point where the two merge, your lack and your plenty combine to create a unique fusion of who you are and what you are capable of. The lack builds into you there, where the plenty may fit. This is your groove. Enjoy your music, or change it.

Success is what you say it is

Avinash Peters, 40, Photographer from Chennai, Runs a café in Kodaikanal

You can hit all the right notes and it might still not be enough. I ran a successful tech company, owned an apartment in Saint Thome in Chennai and drove a Honda City, when, one day, I looked at my pending EMIs and realised this would never end. This was a deep, dark endless abyss. I realised that that was not what I wanted to do in life. So I sold it all and came away to Kodaikanal. At first, it was to think and then I realised that that rat race was not what I wanted to go back to. I took over a café that I had set up with a friend, and began to run it full time. I do freelance photography and I'm currently building my own house.

The need to keep up is everywhere. You don't just want a house, you want it in the right locality. You don't just want a girlfriend, you want the right kind of girlfriend. When you get married, everything is a striving to the picture-perfect marriage. You don't just want a car, you want the right kind of car. It's across sectors. A techie has to have the right kind of laptop. A lot of the issues we face are because we accept these external impositions of what our success, when it eventually comes, will look like. We look for what are the recognisable indicators of our having achieved success. From a relationship to a profession, how do we know we have made it? We use those socially-dictated indicators to decide if we have or not. We rarely know for ourselves, and so everything is an endless keeping up.

If we had to follow our own understanding of what makes us happy, what makes us successful, and what makes us productive and useful, we would be very different people. We would need a whole lot less. And we'd be just fine.

What is success to you? Define that first, before you get yourself into debt over chasing the illusion of it.

♦♦♦

Acknowledgements

"We are never quits with those who oblige us," was Dantes' reply; "for when we do not owe them money, we owe them gratitude."
- The Count of Monte Cristo, Alexander Dumas

Gratitude is owed to Swami, for keeping me focussed on the writing. This book would not have been possible without so many people whose many investments, small and large, tangible and intangible, sustained me. My father, R.I. Jayaraman, who lavished us with everything he had when he had it. My mother, Laxmi Jayaraman, who lavished us with everything we didn't have when we didn't have it. My brother, Gautam Jayaraman, who stepped in with funds, wisdom, advice and patience throughout my trial-and-error of a life. My sister, Gauri Jayaraman, who set such clear paths for herself. And my son, Dhruv, who made all abundance and lack equally irrelevant. My grandmother, Jayalaxmi Venkatraman, for forcing me to buy the gold and insisting I stand on my own two feet. My cousins: Madhu, Sharmi and Charu. Friends and colleagues, Ramya Rajagopalan, R.S. Prakash, Usha Pai, Swati Birla, Hiral Vora, Jamal Shaikh, Kushan Mitra, Kim D'Souza, Priya Thiagarajan, Shantanu Bhattacharya, Sophie Wangkhem, Anmol Choubey, Ravi Krishnan, Khushboo Narayan, Pramit Bhattacharya, Bindisha Sarang, Avanti Shirname, Himanshu Roy, Monisha Raghunathan-Smith and Amrita Raghunathan, P. Rangarajan. To the girls from Anantapur and Saileela madam. To editors and colleagues who sprung me salary advances and created equitable work environments—Priya Ramani,

ACKNOWLEDGEMENTS

R Sukumar, Anil Padmanabhan, Kaveree Bamzai, Kalli Purie, Aroon Purie, Ranjit Sahaya. To Asmita Bakshi, M.G. Arun and Suhani Singh. To Rega Jha, editor of Buzzfeed India, for pushing me to write and for editing the original essay that became the basis for this book and standing like a rock through all the flak it took. To Meru Gokhale, Chitra Duella, Gautam Chikermane, Monika Halan, Amish Tripathi, and Madhavan Narayanan for believing this could be written and connecting the dots to make it so. To advocate Mrunalini Deshmukh for unflinching support. To Bharat Doshi, Bibek Debroy, Ajit Ranade, and a number of unnamed economists for helping me understand context. To Roopa Korde and the faculty and students of Economics, 2016, at FLAME University, Pune. To Avinash Peters for the supply of chocolate cake and fries. So much gratitude to my editor Himanjali Sankar, who gave me a free hand in shaping this book and lent it her quiet, unquestioning support, and to my literary agent Kanishka Gupta for his vocal belief in this book, and the team at Bloomsbury India. And not in the least, to the many contributors who trusted me with the intimate details of the state of their finances and their psychological mind frames, pouring in from Twitter, Facebook, on the streets, in public spaces, at my work desk, to tell their stories. I hope I have done justice to your voices.

May you all be paid back many times over.